END PAPERS

Street Plan, District Six

1. British Cinema
2. Rotten Row
3. National Cinema
4. Ayre Street
5. Caledon Street
6. Hanover Street
7. Seven Steps
8. Horsburg Lane
9. St Mark's Church
10. Muir Street Mosque
11. Clifton Street
12. Star Cinema
13. Aspeling Street
14. Aspeling Street Mosque
15. Dutch Reformed Church
16. Cross Street
17. Lee Street
18. Avalon Cinema

Sandra McGregor

'ONSE ARTIST' IN DISTRICT SIX

DOLORES FLEISCHER

FRONT COVER
Sandra – self-portrait
1965
60 x 50cm
Oil on canvas
Signed bottom right

PRIVATE COLLECTION

I painted this self-portrait in my Military Road flat. The loose orange garment I am wearing was one of Buck's old nightshirts which his wife used to make for him. He took me to District Six for the first time, encouraged me to paint again and opened a new life for me in South Africa.

The photograph of the Indian dancer was a treasured memento of my London days.

First published in South Africa in 2010
Publishing Print Matters (Pty) Ltd
P O Box 640 Noordhoek 7979, Western Cape, South Africa
info@printmatters.co.za • www.printmatters.co.za

Copyright © 2010 Dolores Fleischer

The moral right of the author has been asserted

All rights reserved.
No part of this publication may be reproduced, stored in a retrieval system,
or transmitted, in any form or by any means, without the prior permission
in writing of the publishers or author, nor be otherwise circulated in any form of binding
or cover other than that in which it is published and without a similar condition,
including this condition being imposed on the subsequent purchaser.

A CIP catalogue record for this book is available at the
National Library.

COLLECTORS' EDITION
Limited edition numbered with slipcase
ISBN: 978-0-9814417-0-2
SUBSCRIBERS' EDITION
Hard cover
ISBN: 978-0-9814417-1-9
STANDARD EDITION
Soft cover
ISBN: 978-0-9814417-2-6

EDITORIAL PANEL
Elisabeth Anderson, Robin Stuart-Clark

PICTURE EDITOR
Robin Stuart-Clark

PHOTOGRAPHER
Michael Hall, Cape Town

SCANNING & RETOUCHING
Kirsty Macfarlane

ADDITIONAL PHOTOGRAPHY
Ruphin Coudyzer – Johannesburg
Jeffery Cross – San Franciso
Eyal Gordon – Los Angeles

BOOK DESIGN & FORMATTING
Stuart-Clark & Associates cc, Cape Town, South Africa
Design Drawer cc, Johannesburg, South Africa

PRINTING & BINDING
Craft Print, Singapore

PUBLISHER'S NOTE
Whilst every effort has been made to trace and acknowledge the source and/or ownership of artwork
featured in this book, regrettably some have proved impossible to trace.

Similarly, dating and sizing of artworks is approximate.

In some cases, artwork has been scanned from prints of photographs taken in the 1960s and 70s.
These scans reveal the 'eggshell' texture of the photographic print paper which should not be
interpreted as the texture of canvas or masonite board. Captions of these images are annotated
"Reproduced from photographic print" to avoid any misunderstanding.

*For the wonderful men in my life –
Anthony, Spencer, Lance and Kevin*

A note from the artist

It is a great privilege for any artist to be written about and even more so in his or her own lifetime. Rarer, too, is having my story written by a writer of such warmth and integrity as my friend, Dolores Fleischer.

The contents of this book are as true as my memory serves me. I am grateful to Dolores, for her encouragement, research, and enthusiasm in presenting my life and work to you, and to the publisher, Robin Stuart-Clark, for his dedicated commitment to making a dream come true.

Sandra McGregor
Cape Town
March 2010

Contents

List of Illustrations		2
Preface	The Very Reverend Rowan Q Smith, Dean of Cape Town	5
Foreword	Sandy Prosalendis with Vincent Kolbe	7
PROLOGUE	Finding Sandra	9

PART ONE

CHAPTER 1	Her father's daughter	11
CHAPTER 2	Up and away	19
CHAPTER 3	Steps into Europe	25
CHAPTER 4	Flying with the gods	31
CHAPTER 5	Things fall apart	37
CHAPTER 6	Apprenticeship	51

PART TWO

CHAPTER 7	An open door in Keerom Street	59
CHAPTER 8	Motjie Ragmat's kitchen	71
CHAPTER 9	'Onse artist'	83
CHAPTER 10	The best of times	105
CHAPTER 11	Saturday bioscope	121
CHAPTER 12	Battling the demons	133
CHAPTER 13	My friends the 'skollies'	143
CHAPTER 14	The wrecking ball	163

PART THREE

CHAPTER 15	Beyond the District	175
EPILOGUE	A remarkable heritage	199
Afterword	Sandra McGregor	200
Acknowledgements		201
Appendix 1	Sandra's notes on the basic methods of the old masters and personal colour palette	203
Appendix 2	Sandra's people of District Six	205
Appendix 3	Loyal friends – forty years on	210
List of Collectors and Subscribers		214

List of Illustrations

Chapter 1 – Her father's daughter

10. Lee McGregor and his wife Florence
12. Lee McGregor, 1939
15. Sandra and Davy on board ship at a fancy dress party

Chapter 2 – Up and away

18. Florence and Lee McGregor – *Vaalbos Knop*
21. Lee McGregor

Chapter 4 – Flying with the gods

30. Studio portrait of Sandra
32. Studio portrait of Sandra
32. Studio portrait of Sandra
33. Sandra sketching a young stranger
34. Sandra and Lee McGregor in Rome
35. Sandra in Rome

Chapter 5 – Things fall apart

40. *Portrait of Maria Gloria*
42. *Drawing of Florence in London*
43. *Drawing of Sandra's brother, Davy, in London*
43. Davy with drawing
44. *La Madre – Portrait of Florence McGregor with gold and black shawl*
46. *Portrait of Mr Alexiou, a Cypriot restaurant owner*
48. *Portrait of Paul Asiack, an opera singer*
49. *Portrait of Alan Battenberg, a London lawyer*

Chapter 7 – An open door in Keerom Street

58. Hanover Building, District Six, Cape Town, 1962
59. Buck Jones
61. *Buck's Chair*
62. *Florence in Greenpoint, Cape Town*
63. *Malay Quarter rooftops in sunlight*
63. *Malay Quarter rooftops as the sun is setting*
64. *Malay Quarter rooftops*
65. *The Black Trunk*
66. *Sandra's Kloof Street studio*
67. *Lantern with red background*
68. *Lantern with yellow duster*

Chapter 8 – Motjie Ragmat's kitchen

70. *Portrait of Juleiga*
72. Sandra painting in District Six
76. *Motjie Ragmat's kitchen*
77. *Motjie Ragmat's backyard leading to Caledon Street*
78. *Portrait of Rashied, Motjie Ragmat's grandson*
79. *Portrait of Cass in Hadj robes*
79. *Portrait of Cass with red lantern*
80. *Portrait of Cass*
80. Exhibition Poster featuring *Portrait of Cass*

Chapter 9 – 'Onse artist'

82. Sandra in her studio with exhibition paintings
84. *The Blue Bathroom*
86. *Washline with pigeon loft*
88. *The haunted stair*
90. *Backyard in Caledon Street*
93. *Three Carts*
94. *Life at the Seven Steps – daytime*
95. *Staircase in the 'Big House'*
95. *Stairs with little girl*
96. *Man with broken bottle*
98. *The Seven Steps – woman with curlers*
100. *Sandra's favourite cart*
101. *An old cart*
102. *Vernon Terrace*

Chapter 10 – The best of times

104. Sandra painting in District Six
106. *The Blue Door*
107. *Die Hokke* at the Seven Steps
108. *Portrait of Gadija, an Indian girl*
109. *Backyard behind Hadji's house*
112. *Ayre Street*
112. *Die Kraal, Ayre Street*
112. *Hadji's backyard in bright sunshine*
113. *Atta's kitchen*
113. *Backyard with basins*
115. *Portrait of Charlie*

116. *Portrait of Hadji*
117. *Portrait of Kaye*
118. *Portrait of Duke with hammer*
119. *Portrait of Duke with flagon*

Chapter 11 – Saturday bioscope

120. *The British Cinema*
123. *The British Cinema sideways on*
125. *The National Cinema*
127. Sandra painting the Cross
128. *The Cross for St Cyprian's Anglican Church*
129. *The Cross: detail – Headpiece*
129. *The Cross: detail – Crosspiece*
129. *The Cross: detail – Head of Christ*

Chapter 12 – Battling the demons

132. *Jungian painting 1*
138. *Jungian painting 2*

Chapter 13 – My friends the 'skollies'

142. *Mr Lewis' second-hand shop in Caledon Street*
144. *Balcony scene*
145. *Hanover Lane and Big Sophie*
146. *Hanover Lane scene with chicken*
148. *Rose & Crown Dairy*
150. *Horsburg Lane*
154. *The Field with bicycle boy*
155. *The Field with truck*
156. *National Cinema at night*
158. *A lane between Caledon and Hanover Streets*
162. *St Mark's Church*

Chapter 14 – The wrecking ball

165. Muslim children on their way to the madrasah.
167. *Vasson's Shoe Shop*
168. *Boete Leiman's Fruit and Vegetable Shop*
169. Sandra with children
170. Sandra and young Fareed Rossier
172. *The National Cinema*

Chapter 15 – Beyond the District

174. Sandra in District Six, 2007
175. Canon CT Wood, Senior Chaplain to the Anglican Archbishop of Cape Town
176. *Portrait of Father Robert Mercer, Prior of the Community of the Resurrection*
178. Sandra sketching in St George's Cathedral
178. Christmas Card illustration for St George's Cathedral
179. *Sketch of squatters, St George's Cathedral, Cape Town*
180. *Portrait of the Bishop Suffragan of Cape Town, the Right Reverend Phillip Russell*
182. *Portrait of Dr Reeve Sanders*
183. *Portrait of Carmella Seeff*
184. *Portrait of Dr Maytham*
184. *Portrait of Wendy Maytham*
184. *Portrait of Daniela Capocecera,*
185. Sandra teaching in her studio
186. *The South African Library*
187. *The Kat Balcony*
189. *The Alhambra Theatre*
191. *Wale Street*
193. Letter of permission to paint the prison
194. *Roeland Street Prison*
196. The miniature District Six puppet theatre

Epilogue

198. Sandra McGregor, in the Ladies Christian Home, Cape Town

Appendix 2 – Sandra's people of District Six

205 – 209. District Six Theatre figures

Appendix 3 – Loyal friends – forty years on

211. Aziza, Motjie Ragmat's daughter
211. Sandra and Juleiga, Motjie Ragmat's granddaughter
211. Faldielah, Juleiga's daughter.
211. Sandra and Cass
211. Sandra and Nazima
212. Sandra and Vinod Vasson
212. Sandra and Fareed Rossier

Preface

Steve Biko in the collection of his writings, *I write what I like*, underlines in one of his statements, the importance of recalling our history so that we can live creatively in the present. The divisions, not just of apartheid, but also of our colonial heritage, continue to haunt us so that we do not share a common history as South Africans. Then too, it is said that history records the deeds of the victorious, and the plight of the victims is presented through the eyes of the oppressors.

District Six was not different from any part of the Cape Peninsula but its closeness to the harbour meant that its people, more than anywhere else, reflected what is common to all port cities – a rich tapestry of cultures, ethnic origins and customs. Perhaps it was the vibrance of this community, despite its low economic standards, which made it such a challenge to the apartheid system which sought to create a system of "racial purity" as expressed in the Population Registration Act: "Mixed" was no longer acceptable as a description of "Race." That was the community where Sandra McGregor found an inspiration for her painting and saw herself being designated as "Onse artist" – note even the mixed language - by the local people. There is no desire on her part to patronise the people in the way she interacted with them, nor are her paintings an attempt to create a sentimental view of District Six. Although Vincent Kolbe argues against singling out the Sixth district from the rest of Cape Town, much can be gained by seeing this as representative of all those areas, districts, in the rest of our country whose history was so ruthlessly fragmented by the apartheid system. The people of Loader Street and 'de Waterkant', alongside Strawberry Lane and Constantia come to mind. Sandra McGregor has through her paintings contributed to the rebuilding of the history and the healing of our memories.

Sandra's work did not only focus on District Six nor stop when it was demolished, because in making her 'home' at St George's Cathedral she has in one of her drawings captured the plight of the Crossroads squatters who had taken refuge in the Cathedral, and other places of worship, when their lives and their homes came under attack in 1978. It is often the artist, not only those who paint but also poets and dramatists, who hold up a mirror to us to enable us to see our souls. Sandra McGregor has contributed in her own way to holding up such a mirror and in so doing enabled us to regain what it is to have 'soul'. This book can only but enrich and enhance our overall contribution to recovering our essential soul as South Africans. Thank you Sandra, 'Onse artist.'

The Very Reverend Rowan Q Smith
Dean of Cape Town, 30 March 2010

Foreword

Sandra McGregor, like many people passionate about Cape Town, was not born in the city. Her extraordinary sensitivity is the subject of this book and Dolores Fleischer, whose friendship has stimulated this record of Sandra's life, shares this passion.

Sandra has experienced an intense love affair with the mother city. Her most meaningful paintings are those she did in District Six, an inner part of Cape Town targeted in 1966 for forced removals and demolition by the apartheid government.

An artist in search of place and meaning, she experimented with different styles of painting, but it was here, motivated by her deep love for her friends in the District, that she felt fully human. She did her paintings not to make a political point, she sought no fame, power or notoriety, there was no commercial motive or cleverness in her actions. The reason for painting was simply her feeling of complete 'oneness' with the place and her acceptance by the people. She captured for us what it was like to be a Capetonian in the days before the removals. The part of Cape Town she painted no longer exists, except perhaps in the District Six Museum, and St George's Cathedral, her new home.

When the District was destroyed, Sandra became a lonely woman, almost widowed. Her grief and loss echoed that of the people who were moved out of the city. Vincent Kolbe who writes this foreword with me, remembers that at his Granny's house he never received a letter addressed to District Six as if it was a separate part of Cape Town; letters would come to 121 Aspeling Street, Cape Town. He regrets that we appear to have returned to the apartheid demarcation of District Six, obscuring the unity of what used to be called District Five, Six and Seven. This east end of the inner city was simply Cape Town, and in the interests of citizenship should return to being so.

Dolores Fleischer has worked with Sandra to complete a circle of friendship of over seventy years. She has given us an unusual insight into the personal struggles of a woman born into privilege and contending with love and loss. Hidden from view is Dolores' own testimony of selflessness, kindness and love, those things that are about making us fully human.

Sandy Prosalendis with Vincent Kolbe
Cape Town, 25 February 2010

PROLOGUE

Finding Sandra

In 1995, for the 50th anniversary of leaving Roedean School, Johannesburg, I compiled *Fifty Years On*, a small book of 'life stories' of our class, to mark the occasion. I had not seen Sandra McGregor, one of our class, since a chance meeting in London in 1950. I discovered that she was living in the Ladies' Christian Home in Cape Town, and, subsequently, I collected her from her single room. With long-standing class friends, Barbara, Gill, Peggy, Phil, and Lizzie, we sat together with Sandra to hear the extraordinary story of what had happened in her life during the last half century.

We heard that she had lived in style in London, Paris, and Florence, studying art and sculpture, and had returned to South Africa after many years abroad: how she was bewitched by District Six and how her work there became her life's joy and focus. I found out later that she had been obliged to return from Europe to South Africa. The vagaries and vicissitudes of life had affected her in spite of her early enviable lifestyle and she had suffered disappointment, rejection, loneliness, and poverty.

Sandra painted in District Six from 1962 to 1979. In February 1966, the whole area was declared a 'white area', under the Group Areas Act of 1950, and she witnessed the removals and the breakdown of a community she admired. Her story was inspiring and tragic; her courage and achievements unrecognised. When we found her, she was living alone with her easel and brushes, and a few of her favourite paintings – impecunious, cheerful, and with a lifetime of unrecorded work and experiences.

I was moved by the content of her life's work and the anecdotes she told me. I encouraged her to write down her own story and the history of her paintings. She began over the next few months to fill several small exercise books with free-flowing hand-written memories, and as she talked to me this story began to form. I set about tracking down her works, contacted the descendants of people she had painted, and began to piece it all together.

It was intermittent research, yet over this last decade, Sandra's compelling story has slowly taken shape. I, a stranger to District Six, have recorded it as well as Sandra's recollections and my research dictate. It is one story of many, Sandra's personal view of a place and its people, expressed through her experiences and her paintings, one unique window on District Six. It is a story worth the telling.

Dolores Fleischer
Cape Town, 2010

PART 1

CHAPTER 1

Her father's daughter

Lee McGregor and his wife Florence, taken soon after they were married *circa* 1924, with dachshund, Peggy.

The first child of Alexander Lee McGregor and his wife, Florence, was born in 1928 in a flat in Chudleigh's Building, Eloff Street, Johannesburg. Named Alexandra Hope McGregor, she was always known as Sandra. Her brother, David Ross, was born two years later. Lee McGregor had returned to South Africa after qualifying as a doctor in Edinburgh in 1920. In his early career he worked as a dockhand, storekeeper and gold miner in order to raise funds to study. Subsequently he specialised in surgery, obtaining a Fellowship of the Royal College of Surgeons in London in 1926 and a Mastership in Surgery in Edinburgh in 1927.

In Johannesburg he became a pro bono clinical assistant at the General Hospital and was consulting privately. He was beginning a determined climb to success when Sandra was born. It was clear that he was a brilliant, highly skilled, ambitious man, completely focused on the course he had set for his life.

Florence was born in London but moved to South Africa with her parents. She met Lee McGregor while she was working as a senior theatre sister at the Johannesburg General Hospital. After marrying, they spent almost five years in Chudleigh's, then moved to a small house in Muller Street, Yeoville.

They were living there when the first edition of Lee McGregor's work *A Synopsis of Surgical Anatomy* was published in 1932. He worked laboriously on this book in the early years of marriage. Florence was a source of great strength to her husband, encouraging and helping him in every way. When the book was completed, McGregor took it to the Dean of the Faculty of Medicine at the University of the Witwatersrand, but the University declined to publish the work. This upset him deeply. At the time he was unknown and it was difficult to become established. He was not being sent patients and felt he would never make a success of his career: he even considered giving up medicine.

Florence never doubted his ability and urged him to continue, pressing him to send his book to England. A publisher, John Wright & Sons Limited, Bristol, could barely afford to print the book but took a chance. It certainly paid off, for this useful and popular work ran to eleven editions and twelve reprints by 1975, bringing renown to its author, with substantial royalties. It also brought international recognition to South Africa and today is still used extensively in revised editions.

Later, the family moved to a double-storey house on a small plot in Tudhope Avenue, in the modest but respectable suburb of Berea. Florence and Lee made a serene and secure home for their children. Florence saw to the household and children, freeing her husband to pursue his surgical career. Sandra and Davy were cosseted by their parents who were loving and possessive.

Sandra was accepted at Roedean School, Parktown, considered one of the best schools in Johannesburg. Florence, her gentle, unassuming mother, took Sandra to meet Miss Mackinnon, the headmistress of the Junior School. Sandra recalls that the daunting Rena Mackinnon instructed her to call all teachers 'Madam' – a tradition still in place today. It was the beginning of ten happy years of sound teaching by dedicated teachers at an excellent school. There, Sandra formed friendships which have lasted over decades in spite of long separations. When he was old enough, Davy was sent to St John's College, an equally prestigious boys' school just across the road from Roedean.

During Sandra and Davy's primary school years, Lee McGregor was actively associated with the General Hospital and Witwatersrand University Medical School and was establishing himself as a teacher and anatomist dedicated to the highest standards of surgery.

When I was very young, one of my treats was to accompany my father to the Children's Hospital at Christmas time. My parents had donated a beautiful dolls' house to the hospital where my father was well known and always warmly welcomed. 'Holding father's hand' was one of the great joys in my life as a child.

I recall nothing of the sick children – but only how proud I was of being taken round the wards, holding my father's hand.

In 1939 Lee McGregor was elected President of the Southern Transvaal Branch of the Medical Association of South Africa.

She belonged to him, loved being close to him and felt totally secure when she was with him. She delighted in being called, from time to time, by the special nickname he used for her, 'Sass'.

Sitting on his lap one day at breakfast, my father was eating a fried kipper. He dug out the eyes (considered a delicacy) for me. I remember clearly hearing my mother say, "Why do you spoil her so?"

Spoiling Sandra was to continue for many years.

WHEN SANDRA WAS ABOUT TWELVE, the McGregors bought and settled in a large house with a spacious garden and a tennis court, on Seymour

Avenue in the up-market suburb of Parktown West. This elegant double-storey house was to be home for the children until they were adults.

The McGregors could afford to furnish the house appropriately. In the large entrance hall was a fireplace with a wide grate where a fire was often lit in winter. Two busts, one of Sandra and one of Davy as children, were displayed in the hall. There was also an imposing brass Buddha with a benign smile which stood on an intricately carved black wooden plinth.

> *My early memories of this house are of sitting close beside my father as he read to Davy and me before we went to bed. We all loved Dickens and when I moved into my flat in London many years later, I bought a fine set of Dickens to put upon the bookcase. It made me feel more at home. On cold winter's evenings we would sit before a glowing fire in father's study. Medical literature lined the walls and above the fireplace was a large painting of a naked woman lying on a rug.*

From the age of seven, Florence took Sandra to still life classes with Emily Fern, a delightful old lady. Emily helped Sandra draw and paint, giving her simple instructions and aiding her when necessary. These childish 'works of art' were also displayed on the walls in Lee McGregor's study.

In the drawing-room next to his study hung other paintings and prints, including Alexander Roslin's *The Lady with the Veil,* a colourful study by Stanhope Forbes entitled *Off to the Fishing Ground*, and *Meerlust* by Edward Roworth, depicting the Cape Dutch house 'Meerlust' before a storm. Antique furniture and a French display cabinet containing glass, silver, porcelain and other precious possessions, including The Old Chinaman – a foot-high figure exquisitely carved in ivory – stood in this warm and comfortable room, where guests were entertained. Surrounded by beautiful things, Sandra delighted in them, and her father's desire for her to become an artist was implanted early. Art was to become the crux of her life.

SANDRA'S BEDROOM WAS UPSTAIRS next to her parents' room. A door led onto a balcony overlooking the garden, where she often sat with her father when he came home on summer evenings. Davy's room was on the other side of the house, with a dart board and punch bag. There was a spare room for guests. Another room, opposite the spare room, was used by Florence as a sewing room, and in this room Sandra kept her easel. Here she painted her first portrait.

Books lined the landing and there was a spacious loft, with toys, dolls' prams, large and small dolls, teddy bears, fire engines and other childhood paraphernalia. There was only one general bathroom in this house, and a second small one which was specifically for Sandra's use only. There was a cellar too, but as Lee McGregor drank only gin and tonic or whisky and soda, it was not stocked with wine.

The McGregor family began to entertain more, and staff were employed to help run the house: Magdelene and Charlie indoors, Jack the gardener, and a night-watchman. There was no cook as Florence preferred to do the cooking herself, sometimes helped by Charlie. Charlie, a tall handsome man, waited at table, wearing a white cotton suit, a diagonal red sash and white gloves. In Zulu custom he had large round, multi-coloured earrings in his earlobes. All the staff lived in the servants' quarters at the back of the house.

> *I learnt to bake in the large kitchen, taught by my mother who gave me an American cookery book with colourful illustrations, information on the value of different foods, and menus of all kinds. I recall excitedly writing my name in it.*

Each year at Christmas, the family went to the Cape for a long holiday. They boarded the train at Johannesburg station, the children in their pyjamas and dressing gowns, for the long overnight journey ahead to *Glencrag*, their holiday house in Glencairn near Simon's Town, and the prospect of six weeks with their parents at the seaside. As the family drove through Muizenburg, Sandra and Davy had their first sight of the sea, much to their joy and excitement. As soon as they arrived their father would rush them out to swim in the waves, while their mother was unpacking.

Their father was a deep-sea fisherman and a big-game hunter. On calm days he would take the family out on his boat into the bay. For lunch they would eat fish fresh from the sea, cooked on the boat by their mother. Once a week the family drove into Cape Town to buy fresh fruit on the Grand Parade. The McGregors took annual six-week holidays for many years, and when Sandra was living overseas, she would come back to join them.

THE MCGREGORS took Sandra and Davy to England by sea before World War Two, when they were relatively young. This was a popular trip in the mid-thirties, when sea travel was delightful.

In 1940 they took a trip to America by air, flying across Africa and the Atlantic, to avoid the Battle of Britain. America did not enter the war until December 1941, and Lee McGregor specifically wanted to meet a famous

Sandra as a Christmas cracker and Doctor Davy in a fancy dress parade aboard ship.

surgeon, Reginald Smithwick, in Boston. The plane refuelled at Kano in northern Nigeria, and in the hotel, watching huge spiders on the ceiling, Sandra was terrified. She also argued with Davy as to who should sit next to her father on the long flight: Davy won. Sandra recalls that they stayed at prestigious hotels – the Statler Hotel in Boston and the Waldorf Astoria in New York. The highlight of the whole trip for Sandra, who was then about thirteen, was being given her first full length fur coat by her parents. It was bought in Boston and was of wonderful heavy, beaver skin. She wore it for over twenty years.

Dr Smithwick was noted for his development of the Smithwick Operation, used for controlling hypertension before drugs were readily available. Lee McGregor showed remarkable foresight in making this contact, and on his return to Johannesburg was the first to offer this surgical method of controlling high blood pressure. It brought him patients from far and wide.

Lee McGregor's rise in the medical world was indeed a remarkable success story. His concomitant financial success enabled him to live in style in Johannesburg, to own a holiday house and boat in the Cape, and also to become a serious Africander stud farmer. Later, Davy managed this huge cattle farm for his father.

The McGregor household reflected solid prosperity and respectability: a distinguished surgeon, recognised worldwide, a supportive wife, two children at expensive private schools, acceptance in Johannesburg society, and no dark secrets at all.

IN DECEMBER 1945, at the end of the school year, the family went on holiday to Glencrag and returned home, as usual, on the Blue Train. Sandra's results were awaiting her: a First Class Matriculation! She had worked hard to make her father proud of her. The whole family was excited, but her father's praise was what she desired most. He took her to the Lady Dudley Nursing Home where he consulted, and proudly told the doctors, nurses and the indispensible Matron Watson of his daughter's success.

It had been decided that Sandra should spend nine months at home before leaving for Europe to start her art studies in the autumn. It was holiday time and she and her contemporaries were growing up: tennis parties, dances in private houses – where young guests were formally introduced to the parent hosts – dances at the Country Club chaperoned by her parents; young men coming into her life. It all made for an exciting round of enjoyment and fun. The war was over, soldiers had returned from 'Up North', eager to resume normal life again. Sandra began to have admirers and to care about her appearance.

Sandra had been plump as a child but in her late teens she decided she must lose weight and began to eat less. She dropped from Size 16 to Size 12. Her father said she looked like a skeleton and her mother was very concerned. There was a surgical congress in Lourenço Marques in 1946, which her father was to attend. Sandra and her parents motored down to Moçambique and stayed at the luxurious Polana Hotel. She was very slim and proud of her figure by then, and her mother had bought her some lovely new clothes which Sandra wore with great pleasure.

However, she began to feel ill from lack of food, but at the same time craved sweets and cakes. A doctor, a friend of her father, told her that she had better start eating normally or else "she would resort to tickling her throat with a peacock feather". She did not know what he meant, but the remark lodged in her mind. Sandra ended her starvation diet shortly before leaving to live in London, and once there, her anorexic condition disappeared.

Florence hid her sadness at Sandra's imminent departure. She knew how spell-binding London would be for her and feared she would never return to live in South Africa.

I recall my mother complaining to my father, "You are taking my daughter away from me." In anticipation at the prospect of being in London, I did not give it much thought.

Sandra shared with her father her excitement about all she would see in London: the National Gallery, the Tate, the Wallace Collection, the Imperial War Museum, and the British Museum. He told her about famous London theatres, about Hampton Court and Stratford-upon-Avon. Many of these and other attractions, particularly the National Portrait Gallery, were to become part of Sandra's everyday London life.

By 1946, when Lee McGregor was making plans for Sandra's departure for London, he was, at fifty-two, one of the most sought-after and versatile surgeons in Johannesburg. He had a dignified, immaculate appearance, always wearing a stiff pointed collar and bow tie, and was a great disciplinarian, strictly punctual, and a perfectionist. He could be sarcastic with those who did not measure up to his standards and his attitude may have been interpreted as arrogant. At home he was a domineering *pater familias*: they all did as they were told.

In the same year, Matron Watson appointed a new theatre sister at the Dudley Nursing Home, an appointment that she would come to regret.

◆

CHAPTER 2

Up and away

Florence and Lee McGregor on their cattle farm, Vaalbos Knop, in the Vryburg district.

Plans were in place. It was time for Sandra to leave. World War Two was over and, to many people's delight, air travel between South Africa and Europe had been introduced. The McGregors decided not to go by sea but to fly to London. The low-flying, slow, unpressurised planes, Skymasters or Vickers Vikings, flew overland up Africa before crossing into Europe or England, requiring at least three refuelling and rest stops on the way. The whole journey took about 36 hours: much faster than the mail boat from Cape Town to Southampton, a leisurely two week cruise.

Departure was from Palmietfontein – a small airport which served Johannesburg until 1952 – and routes varied. Landings were made at little known but convenient and friendly places such as Kisumu on Lake Victoria, Khartoum in the Sudan, and Castel Benito, a former Royal Air Force base, now Tripoli International Airport in Libya.

Sandra, on the many trips she made between South Africa and Europe, never travelled by sea again, only by air.

Once in London, Sandra and her parents stayed at the Cadogan Hotel, off Sloane Square. Two matters had to be finalised: where would Sandra study and where would she live? With the help of a Roedean friend, Monica Rissik, a suitable place for Sandra to lodge was found, with a lawyer and his family in their house on the Putney embankment. Sandra was to have a room upstairs with a much appreciated view of the Thames – especially during the Oxford-Cambridge boat race.

Heatherley's School of Fine Art had been recommended by Louise Rissik, Monica's sister. It was a leading and well established art school in Warwick Square. An interview was arranged.

My parents and I entered an old Victorian house with an imposing staircase in the entrance hall, and were taken to meet Gordon Eames who ran Heatherley's. We were shown into his office where a fire was burning and he greeted us in his carpet slippers. He appeared to me as a character straight from Dickens. His secretary, Miss Cooper, ('Coops' as he called her) brought in the tea. Rumour had it that 'Coops' was Mr Eames's mistress.

Examples of Sandra's work had been sent from South Africa, and on the basis of these and the interview she was accepted by the school. The McGregors were shown around the building: the life room where students studied drawing from life; the still life room upstairs, with shelves of interesting objects and plaster casts, was also used for portraiture. Sandra noticed the large high windows and the spacious bright rooms. Later, in winter, she was disappointed to discover that it was necessary to work by electric light. Her parents were delighted with their choice of art school, and had high expectations of all that she would be taught there.

Sandra's parents supervised their daughter's move into her Putney room, and then left for a surgical congress in Scotland, before travelling to America. Only when they departed, did Sandra realise what living away from them was going to mean. She had never been separated from her parents, not been a boarder at Roedean, never gone away without them nor lived on her own anywhere, certainly not in a strange, unfamiliar metropolis.

> *They phoned me that evening from Edinburgh. I cried and cried and cried – and counted the days for their return. Oh the joy when they did! I remember what they brought me: several pairs of the loveliest mittens I had ever seen; ear-muffs against the cold; beautiful sweaters – and a large basket of delicious Canadian apples.*

HEATHERLEY'S, FOUNDED IN 1845, the oldest independent art school in London and the first school to admit women on equal terms with men, focused on portraiture, figurative painting and sculpture. Edward Burne-Jones, Dante Gabriel Rossetti, John Everett Millais, William Russell Flint and Walter Sickert were former students, as was the first Principal of the Slade School of Art, Sir Edmund Poynter, and the first Principal of the Royal College of Art, Walter Crane.

The two established professors of art in the school when Sandra arrived there, were gifted teachers: Frederick Whiting, RA who taught Sandra portraiture, and Iain McNab who took the life-drawing class. Iain and his wife, Helen, became good friends of Sandra's. Iain, with a short beard and broad Scottish accent, always wore a blue artist's smock. Helen, a dancer, went to South Africa to dance, and stayed for a while with Sandra's parents. Another teacher, Frank Wynne-Thomas, shy and reserved, taught still life and portraiture. He also became a friend, and later visited her Chelsea studio, where she appreciated his helpful criticism.

These teachers, artists themselves, gave Sandra the basics of life drawing, still life, and portraiture. They did not teach special techniques, but focused on the fundamentals of drawing as the basis for any art work.

It was post-war London and food was still rationed. Sandra's mother

Sandra's father, Lee McGregor.

sent her food parcels – tinned hams, boxes of prunes from the United States, fruit, and other delicacies unobtainable in London at the time. Not all of these reached her, most of them went into her landlord's household larder.

Sandra was lonely at first without the closeness and comfort of her family, and virtually no friends. Communication was mainly by hand-written letters. Telephoning was expensive and long-distance calls had to be pre-arranged. She wrote pages and pages to her parents on all that she was seeing, doing and learning in England. Her parents re-lived London through these letters, and loved hearing from her. She wrote every week and so did they.

IN THE TENSE and over-charged atmosphere of an operating theatre a surgeon works closely with all those involved: people become attracted to other people, long marriages may become boring, the so-called 'mid-life crisis' occurs, new relationships are formed. The new theatre sister, Agnes Stevenson, had proved an excellent appointment, and in due course she arranged matters to ensure that she was always present in theatre when Lee McGregor was operating. For him, what may have started as a passing affair – he was known to have had several – became an over-riding passion.

A popular surgeon, at the peak of his career, he was out by eight every morning, and came back to a quiet home in the evening. After his affair blossomed, Agnes Stevenson's small flat at Clarendon Circle became a second destination in the late evening. Sandra's 51 year-old mother, her children away, her house empty, had no guile with which to fight the disaster which had overtaken her. Three years passed like this. Sandra was unaware of the situation – unaware of her mother's pain and her prayers that God would end the affair. When Sandra returned to Johannesburg on holiday, she noticed nothing wrong – her father was always particularly careful, and her mother said nothing.

> On one of these visits, I had a small operation to my foot at the Lady Dudley Nursing Home. Agnes Stevenson sent flowers to my ward, with a get-well card, and came to sit with me. As we talked I said, "How strange it is that you have never married." Agnes in return asked me why I had never thought of marriage. "I love my father so much that I shall never marry unless I meet a man exactly like him."
>
> "Until I meet a man exactly like your father, I shall not marry either," Agnes replied.

Sandra thought nothing of this at the time.

WHEN SANDRA CAME HOME from Europe each year her life was filled with pleasure: the tennis parties and dances continued, the frivolous round of enjoyment was in full swing. Lee McGregor was a good tennis player and often invited young doctors and registrars to play on their tennis court at home. Florence always ensured a substantial tea was served and Sandra enjoyed the company. At the Country Club on Saturday nights, in spite of attentive young men, Sandra still preferred dancing with her father. She loved the embrace of his strong arms holding her close to him. He was a good dancer and, as she had as a child when holding his hand in the hospital, she felt the same security, love and admiration while spinning with her handsome father on the ballroom floor.

Randle Barlow, son of McGregor's friend Dr Lancelot Barlow, was attracted to Sandra and they went out together frequently when she was home. She enjoyed Randle's company and her mother liked him. She hoped Sandra would marry him one day. Her father, however, disliked him intensely and could not bear to see Sandra dancing with him. Sandra was fond of Randle but was not in love with him, and was alarmed when he proposed: she was certainly not interested in marriage, and in any case knew that her father would say 'No' at once.

> *My father had told me firmly that I should never marry, but should concentrate on my art. He also told me that having an affair out of wedlock was the biggest sin a woman could commit. Besides, marrying and living in Johannesburg played no part in my life. I was too self-centred even to think of Randle's feelings, or of my mother's sadness, for she missed me greatly when I was away. Dancing round the world with never a care was what I enjoyed most.*

SANDRA'S PARENTS, visiting London in 1948, did not like Sandra walking alone, often in the dark, from Putney. They moved her to a big house in Queensgate, run by Commander Meredith. There she had a room, bathroom and meals provided, and was closer to Heatherleys.

> *I spent four happy years, 1947-1950, at Heatherley's. I made friends there, some rich from titled families, and others like John, who had talent but was hard-up. John often asked for the oil paint I scraped off my palette at the end of the day. There were also three ex-servicemen, one, a man whose legs had been amputated above the knees: he drove his own car, and managed to climb and descend the stairs to the life-drawing room.*

> *With one friend, Esmé Held, talented and full of fun, I went to see a play in Stratford-upon-Avon and we spent the night there. With another, Diana Bard, unspoiled by the wealth of her titled parents, I frequented a workmen's café for lunch: incredibly cheap, but very good value – we had delicious jam roll for dessert quite often. I often wondered what her family thought of us.*

Some of these friends celebrated Sandra's 21st birthday with her on the 2nd of October 1949, at a dance at the Savoy Hotel. The party was hosted by a colleague of her father and his wife, Sir Heneage and Lady Ogilvie. They had been house guests of the McGregors when visiting South Africa for a surgical congress. Sandra's mother sent her a white lace dress from 'Rejane', an exclusive dress shop in Johannesburg. Unfortunately her parents were unable to travel to London for this celebration: her father was too busy and her mother would never have gone alone.

Lee McGregor's name opened many doors, and he wanted Sandra to be introduced to his London colleagues, particularly his friend Lord Webb-Johnson. Sandra had attended several monthly dinners at the Royal College of Surgeons with her parents, but later she was asked on her own. It was customary for a visitor to give a short speech and at one event Lord Webb-Johnson asked Sandra to speak. She spoke about the thrill of living in London, and about her studies at Heatherley's and the work she was doing. She met doctors, physicians and surgeons, many of whom were kind to her, but none had the charisma of her father. On one occasion, when her father was present at a dinner party given by Lady Webb-Johnson in Portland Place, EP Scott, a physician and friend, turned to Sandra and said, *sotto-voce*, "For goodness sake take your eyes off your father and look at some other man instead!"

When she flew home on holiday her parents would be waiting for her and it was into her father's arms that she ran. That was where she wanted to be. Only later did Sandra realise how much she had hurt her mother, but Florence accepted this as she was to accept so much more. Her father was her whole life and, as at school, she did everything to make him proud of her. She had no financial restrictions or concerns. She knew her father would always provide for her.

> *My father was to me the most wonderful man I had ever met.*
> *There was a very special feeling between us. I had met many men in my life, but none of them ever compared to my father. He was a*

man of great authority, extremely well read, a lovely sense of humour, wonderful to talk to concerning Europe and all my activities there. But not quite all my activities. I did not tell him of the operas and ballets and plays I saw, and the men that invited me to them. I knew that there was only one man in my life and that was himself – he took that for granted.

◆

CHAPTER 3

Steps into Europe

After four years at Heatherley's Sandra felt that she had absorbed all that she could from its teaching. She was interested in Rembrandt's paintings and techniques, and as her father was going to Amsterdam in 1951 on a medical congress, he suggested she accompany him. Since 1885, the Rijksmuseum containing Rembrandt's work, had been housed in architect Pierre Cuypers' imposing building on the Museumplein square, in the heart of Amsterdam. Sandra and her father were disappointed, however, to find that no post-war students were permitted to copy the masterpieces. The paintings had not been retrieved from the cellars where they had been stored during World War Two.

The Frans Hals Museum in Haarlem was suggested instead, and to Sandra's delight her father then arranged for her to copy his paintings. Sandra knew and admired his famous work, *The Laughing Cavalier*, which typifies his extraordinary skill.

Her father also arranged for her to live in the well known Park Hotel, close to Vondel Park, where for almost a year she had a bedroom, sitting room and bathroom. Every weekday she walked to the station, caught a train to Haarlem, and walked to the museum.

I was so mad on painting that I decided to copy all the cavaliers
I admired most. Some of the paintings were of five or more seated
at a table. They gave me a strong ladder and I had no qualms in
mounting it and copying the debonair laughing men in their
beautiful costumes of silk or satin or lace. I copied about thirty-five
paintings of cavaliers in all.

The Park Hotel was not far from the Amsterdam home of Dr Elise Sanders, a friend of Lee McGregor and the first female gynaecologist in Holland. Elise was a cultured woman, an authority on art and music, who shared her extensive knowledge with Sandra. They became friends and Sandra dined with her, often twice a week.

Sandra and her father were invited to dine with a Dutch surgeon, Professor Nuboer. He had young sons and Sandra would later spend weekends with the Nuboer family who were always kind to her. She never met the professor's wife who had moved to the country during the war, and did not return to the city.

THROUGH THE NUBOERS, Sandra was introduced to Willem Wolffensperger, a young doctor. Sandra was attractive to men, with her long flowing dark hair, bright eyes and neat figure, and she needed company of her own age.

Sandra and Wim started going out together. He had very little money but that did not seem to matter, and they became fond of one another. On Friday and Saturday evenings they had simple meals and then went dancing. On weekends they often went on excursions to centres such as Vollendam or Marken; to towns where excellent cheeses were produced; to the museums in Amsterdam. They went for walks alongside the canals and walks on the beach to Sandvoort. Sandra did not tell her parents about Wim, and during the week continued drawing and painting in the Frans Hals Museum.

Elise Sanders realised there was someone in Sandra's life and asked to meet him. Wim was slim, good-looking with dark eyes, and very likeable, but for some reason Elise took a dislike to him and she refused to see him again. This became awkward for Sandra, who continued going out with him, and in due course he asked her to marry him. At the same time he told Sandra that he had been married and divorced during the war when working at a hospital in Indonesia.

> *I was horrified. He begged me to understand. But with my father's attitude to divorce, I knew what he would say. This cast a shadow over our relationship.*

When Sandra returned home on holiday she told her parents about Wim, and said she was very fond of him, adding that he wanted to marry her. She also mentioned that he had little money and was divorced.

Her father's reaction was predictable. What right had any man to ask Sandra to marry him when he could not support her in the manner to which she was accustomed? That a divorced man should want to marry her was scandalous! Sandra was to end the relationship immediately. As always, she did what her father told her, and on her return to Europe felt obliged to break up with Wim, regardless of his feelings.

Divorce in those days was severely frowned upon. It was something 'nice' people did not do. Men may have had mistresses, but to maintain the façade of marriage and the family was paramount. Divorced people were often shunned, or dropped from society altogether. Sandra's father had made it clear over the years that he was against divorce.

IT WAS TIME TO MOVE ON. Sandra wanted to see Paris and to attend a French art school. Her father arranged for her to study at the Académie

Julien, a private atelier in Paris. Both she and her father believed that an artist's training was not complete without copying paintings in the Louvre, and absorbing the Masters.

The Académie Julien was established in 1868, at which time the École des Beaux-Arts, the government-sanctioned art school of France, did not allow women to enrol. Like Heatherley's, the new Académie Julien admitted women and they participated in the same studies as men, including the basis of art training at the time – drawing and painting of nude models – previously considered improper for women. In London, female models posed nude, but not male models. Men wore 'trunks' or a strategically placed cloth. On her first morning at Académie Julien a male model posed entirely naked: the other English girls and Sandra looked embarrassed, so the French professor said to the model, in French, "Turn around with your back to that group over there – they are English!"

In Paris Sandra lodged in the house of Madame Grellou, in the Rue Arsene Houssaye, off the Champs Elysées – a wonderfully central location. Sandra could live there comfortably and her father's money gave her a certain self-confidence. A vase of red roses awaited her with a loving card from Wim on the morning she reached Paris, but he visited her there only once.

In addition to the French who studied there, the Académie Julien was popular with Americans and other foreign students. Sandra recalls the class gathered round a slim student, who showed them marks tattooed on her arm – marks from the German concentration camp which she had survived.

SANDRA IMMERSED HERSELF IN PARIS. She travelled all over the city by bus or on foot. Alone, or occasionally with a friend, she saw all she could: she loved Montmartre, the artists' quarters and studios; the churches and cathedrals, the stained glass windows; Saint-Germain-des-Prés, Versailles and all the great monuments outside Paris; the haute couture shows and the latest fashions, and Paris by night. But most of all she loved the art galleries and collections, and the museums. She admired the Impressionists and spent long days on her own absorbing their works.

Despite this, Florence, Rome and Venice would come to mean much more to her – not only the cities but the towns and villages, and in due course the Italian people. She found them much warmer and more vivacious than the French, whom she said were cold and unfriendly. She felt Parisians generally were not welcoming to foreigners, and often hostile or contemptuous of people who could not speak French.

The work at the Académie Julien was similar to that at Heatherley's and Sandra soon realised that they could not teach her more than she had learnt in London. She drew from life, but mainly studied portraiture, painting models the school provided. Sandra kept no work from Paris other than three portraits, one of an old Frenchman with a beard, his hands resting on his cane, the other two of models at the Académie Julien. Nor did Sandra copy any of the old masters in the galleries.

DURING THIS TIME Sandra went back to Amsterdam once only, to visit Elise Sanders who was very ill, and she stayed with her for a short time. She did not see Wim. From there she flew home for her annual holiday and never returned to Paris.

One of Sandra's journeys was on the last flying boat 'down Africa' in November 1950. In May 1948, BOAC introduced Short Solent flying boats on the UK-Johannesburg service. The route was Southampton – Augusta (Sicily) - Cairo - Luxor - Khartoum - Port Bell - Victoria Falls - Vaaldam. The planes flew slowly and were very comfortable, and of course could only land on water. It was gracious travelling, and the journey took four days from start to finish.

The seats were spacious and passengers could walk freely about the aircraft. There were two decks, with a bar and sitting rooms on the upper deck. Take-off was at nine o'clock in the morning and landing about four in the afternoon, when the passengers disembarked for the overnight stop. In Luxor passengers were taken to the Palace Hotel on the Nile and slept in huge beds under mosquito nets in palatial rooms – a full moon and exotic music adding to the magic. Victoria Falls was another fascinating stop: the plane landed on the Zambezi River above the Falls and the passengers were then taken by road to the elegant and historic colonial Victoria Falls Hotel for the night. There was time to pass Livingstone's statue, to see the gorge in all its thundering majesty and the bridge which was part of Cecil John Rhodes' dream of the Cape to Cairo railway. Sandra was enthralled by it all.

BEFORE LEAVING FOR ITALY, Sandra's father said he had something to tell her. She was not at all prepared for the bombshell he dropped.

He told Sandra that he had previously been married when studying for his medical degree in Edinburgh. There had been two daughters by that marriage, Beatrice and Anne. When he returned to South Africa he supported them financially, until he divorced his first wife. Then he sent them a final lump sum and there was little further communication. He asked Sandra not to tell Davy.

I was astonished that my beloved father could have kept this secret from me all my life. I was then twenty-four. How could he have done this? I had two grown-up half-sisters whom I had never known about, never met! My father had been married and divorced! Why hadn't my mother told me? Why was my father so against my marrying Wim, when he himself had been divorced? The questions went around in my head endlessly.

But, like other unpleasant matters, Sandra suppressed them and did not talk about them. Her adoration for her father overcame any obstacle which might affect their relationship.

Much later, Sandra's mother told her that Beatrice had become a good artist, but found it hard to make a living. She had married a struggling sculptor, and subsequently earned her living as an art teacher. Anne had followed her vocation as a missionary. Later, Lee McGregor had received a letter from the hospital where Anne lay dying. He did not respond.

Soon after this revelation, Lee McGregor asked Florence for a divorce.

◆

Sandra McGregor – 'Onse artist' in District Six

CHAPTER 4

Flying with the gods

Studio portrait of Sandra by Lumachi, a notable photographer of Florence.

The night Sandra was to fly to Rome, a grateful patient of her father, a businessman by the name of Malcolm Smith, presented her with a beautiful black leather handbag and asked if she could carry with her a fur stole for his wife Elda, an opera singer living in Milan. On arriving at the hotel in Rome, Sandra realised her handbag was missing. In it were keys, money, introductions to certain Italians and Elda's address.

Leaving my luggage and stole with the porter, I rushed out into the street where, in the distance, I saw two taxis. The driver of the first thought it ridiculous to try and find the taxi whose driver had deposited me at my hotel. Calling on God to help me, I rushed to the other taxi and there on the floor was my handbag. The driver had not noticed it.

From Rome, Sandra took the train to Florence, delivered the stole to Elda Ribetti, and met Elda's parents, Colonel Ribetti and his wife, who were to become her friends. Elda was slim, beautiful, with red hair and green eyes. Sandra spent many weekends with her, and attended some of her performances.

Sandra immediately liked the friendliness and vivacity of the Italians and made friends wherever she went. Her pensione, Albergo Balestri, was on the banks of the Arno not far from the Ponte Vecchio. In every direction the beauty was breath-taking: the terracotta tiles of the rooftops of Florence; the shops with their superb leather goods; across the Arno the leather-workers who made purses, wallets, belts and handbags of all styles and colours. The market close by sold straw goods and Sandra found the bags most useful for her art equipment. The shops on the Ponte Vecchio displayed collections of jewellery, dresses, and hand-made shoes fashioned by unknown craftsmen. Sandra was amazed at how little the shoes cost. Italian friends insisted, however, that she wear shoes by master craftsman Ferragamo. Ferragamo's shop sold sandals on one floor, day shoes on the next, and in the salon above that, evening shoes. Sandra had two pairs of evening shoes made for her: they fitted perfectly.

SANDRA KNEW SHE WAS PRIVILEGED. All her expenses were paid by her father who also gave her an allowance every month that more than provided for everything she acquired. His generous financial support made possible the luxury she enjoyed, the clothes she bought, and her travels through Italy. She did not have to earn her living. The level on which she lived was high – but as natural to her as the air she breathed.

I owe to my beloved father the opportunities he gave me – far from Johannesburg – of drinking deeply from the wine of life, so that I flew with the gods and lived with the gods.

She often lunched with Colonel Ribetti and his wife on Sundays in their comfortable Florentine house. Signor and Signora Alberto Magni, who had a penthouse on the banks of the Arno, also became friends. Alberto was a cloth manufacturer, whose charm, understanding, ability and talents were widely admired. His wife, Stella, an Italian beauty with a splendid dress sense, was also a successful sculptress. Sandra often stayed with Stella in the Magni's house in Bari, on the South East coast of Italy, and on one visit she attended a magnificent ball there.

Alberto Magni opened a similar fabric business in South Africa and later Stella lived mainly in Johannesburg where she frequently exhibited her sculpture, painting and jewellery. Initially she painted delicate watercolours and later produced vigourous bronze sculptures – a bushman running, a Moçambican fisherman, elegant Xhosa women. She also produced a bronze figure of the Pope in full papal regalia which was presented to Pope John Paul II.

Sadly, Sandra and Stella's lives never crossed in South Africa.

SANDRA ENROLLED at the Accademia delle Belle Arti in Florence, where she painted portraits in oil and worked in pencil and crayon, and pen and ink. The great masters were more compelling however, and she spent many hours studying their work. She soon left the Accademia, which she felt was teaching her the same things she had learnt at Heatherley's. Instead Sandra chose to draw in museums, cathedrals and market places. Wherever she went there were subjects to draw and paint and she filled many sketch books. She lived with Rembrandt, Titian and Tintoretto, Canaletto, Botticelli and Mantegna and many others. Her world was filled with their masterpieces, their colours, their inspiration.

She spent a week in the ancient town of Assisi, in Umbria, birth place of St Francis who founded the Franciscan religious order there in 1208. She visited the two medieval castles which dominate the town, and wandered through the Basilicas of San Francesco d'Assisi and of Santa Chiara (St Clare), absorbing the frescoes and architecture. Many years later, Sandra was to base one of her works on the Cross of St Francis of Assisi.

Above and below: studio pictures of Sandra by Lumachi.

Sandra sketching a young stranger, in a café in Florence.

Sandra was free to travel from one end of Italy to the other. Robert Browning's famous quotation – placed on the façade of Ca' Rezzonico, the baroque palazzo in Venice where he died in 1899 and now the museum of 18th century Venice – sums up her love for Italy: 'Open my heart and you will see graven inside of it Italy!'

DINO MISCHI, A LAWYER and friend of Alberto Magni, began to escort Sandra regularly. He took her to many places she longed to see: Verona, Vicenza and Venice, Capri and Ischia. Her mother had given her a beautiful edition of Axel Munthe's *The Story of San Michele*, and she eagerly anticipated a scene described in the book. Suddenly there it was right in front of her: the Bay of Naples and the Villa San Michele.

In Capri, we took a boat trip to the mysterious Blue Grotto. In a rough sea, the boatman watched the movement of the water, waiting for the appropriate moment to catch hold of the chain attached to the vault of the entrance, in order to pull the rowing boat into the cave. It was dark and we could see nothing, until he bent over the boat and tossed handfuls of the water into the air - and silver and golden stars came sparkling down.

In Venice, a city Sandra had often studied in photographs, they travelled in gondolas, sight-seeing. Sandra was ecstatic. She stared up at the imposingly beautiful Basilica di Santa Maria della Salute, its soaring dome silhouetted against the blue Italian sky; explored its expansive interior, gasped at the breath-taking Baroque high altar, the paintings of Tintoretto and Titian. They visited the short Bridge of Sighs, immortalised by Lord Byron in his poem, *Childe Harold's Pilgrimage*: "I stood in Venice on the Bridge of Sighs, a palace and a prison on each hand." Sandra recalled a Gwelo Goodman painting of it in their Johannesburg home.

> *In the Piazza San Marco where we dined, I ordered a speciality soup. When I stirred it catfish tentacles – considered a great delicacy in Venice – came to the surface! I hastily ordered something else.*

Sandra with her father in Rome. Sandra remarked that her father appears troubled and sad.

Socially her life was full. People she met understood she had no need to earn a living. She and Dino enjoyed fine restaurants, and on terraces in summer they danced beneath the Italian night sky to the love songs of Italy. He had become her constant companion, and, in due course, asked Sandra to marry him. With his money and hers, he said, they could live a very good life together. Sandra had grown very close to Dino. Her father had told her many times that marriage would interfere with the fulfilment of her artistic promise. Once again, for love of her father, Sandra reluctantly ended a relationship which she knew she could not maintain without his permission and support. Her father was still controlling her and directing her life from afar, making it impossible for any other man to take his daughter from him.

IN FLORENCE Sandra had been introduced to a charming Italian woman, Margherita Patrucci and her husband, Gualtiero. She moved to Margherita's residence, the Pensione la Cupola, then only recently opened. She had a room and bathroom and with other guests enjoyed the cooking of Mario, the chef. Her shutters, closed at night, were flung open early each morning to the view of Brunelleschi's Duomo, the Cathedral of Florence. Across the road was the Batistero di San Giovanni, an octagonal construction from the early eleventh century built over Roman ruins, with famous golden doors by Lorenzo Ghiberti.

A short walk led her to the Piazza della Signoria and then to the Uffizi Gallery where, upstairs, she came to the Botticelli Gallery, which held two of the world's greatest masterpieces, *La Primavera* and the *Nascita di Venere*. She was privileged to see these paintings alone in an empty gallery, since in those early post-war years there were few tourists out of season.

Sandra painted portraits of many people who came and went at the Pensione La Cupola, giving away most of them to her sitters. She never charged for any of her work, and kept only a few of these canvases.

Margherita's sister, Gigi, used a very good dressmaker, and like Alberto Magni, Gigi's husband ran a fabric business. Sandra set about choosing cloth for each season of the year and had an entire wardrobe of Italian clothes made. She had studied Italian grammar and pronunciation informally while in London, but in Italy she spoke Italian only, becoming fluent. As the years passed she began to feel Italian, and always dressed in the Italian way. Twice she went to London to see her friends, who no doubt noticed how well-dressed she was. They noticed too her profound happiness.

The beauty of Italy! For me it remains the most marvellous country in the world.

AN OPPORTUNITY AROSE for Sandra to take private classes with Primo Conti, a well-known Italian portrait painter. Conti was then in his fifties and was to become a major figure of Italy's Futurist school of painting. His house, formerly a fifteenth century monastery on the slopes of Fiesole, had a panoramic view of the Tuscan landscape. His wife was a young English woman who had gone to Italy to study under him. They had fallen in love and married, and thereafter she helped him in his classes, cleaning his brushes and palette.

Sandra in Rome.

Sandra and a talented Indian girl, Himu, who was also studying with Conti, painted each other's portraits and Sandra also painted a portrait of Primo Conti's seventeen year-old daughter, Maria Gloria. At Conti's house Sandra met Pietro Annigoni, ten years younger than Primo Conti and a friend of his. Acclaimed as a painter of royalty, Annigoni's subjects were drawn from a wide cross-section of people: Pope John XXIII, the Shah of Iran, the ballet legend Margot Fonteyn, the famous shoemaker Salvatore Ferragamo. In particular it was his commissioned 1956 portrait of Her Majesty Queen Elizabeth II, which brought both the portrait and Annigoni tremendous fame.

The Primo Conti Foundation was created in the 1980s, thanks to Conti's donation of this house, his archives and his works of art, 'to preserve the memory and testimonials of the most important innovating movements in the twentieth century.' Over 60 oil paintings and 150 drawings by Primo Conti are on display in the Museum which was opened to the public in 1987.

Everywhere Sandra went in Italy she was met by kindness, hospitality and goodwill. Those five years, from 1952 until late 1956, were filled with such beauty, such revelations of great art, architecture and sculpture that she was enchanted by the magic of it all. Her interest in Buddhism and reincarnation convinced her that in some other lifetime she had lived in Italy, that there were places and people she had seen or known before. In La Cupola where she lived, an Italian woman remarked that Sandra never looked sad or worried, and Sandra's reply reflected her happiness.

Mia Signora, io sono felice, io non ho nessun problema!

At no stage could Sandra have anticipated that her happiness and life without problems was soon to be shattered.

CHAPTER 5

Things fall apart

While Sandra was in Italy her father's mistress, Agnes Stevenson, moved into the family home in Johannesburg, and Sandra's mother, Florence, moved out to live on the large McGregor cattle ranch, *Vaalbos Knop*, which her son, Davy was running. Sandra was recalled to South Africa while this was happening. It was a time of great sadness and upheaval for her mother, herself and Davy. Her father met her at the airport as usual, but told her that he had booked a room for her at the Carlton Hotel: Agnes did not want her living 'at home'. This came as a terrible shock.

Davy took his mother to gather up a few of her own possessions from her former home. Charlie met them at the door. "Oh madam, are you coming home?"

"No Charlie, I would give my life if that was so."

Florence took little with her, saying that she did not want to upset her husband. She did not even take her precious dachshunds which she adored. Much later, Sandra acknowledged that both she and her mother were afraid of her father, which accounts for their meek reaction. Sandra was instructed by her father to clear her mother's cupboards to make way for Agnes's clothes. She was told to do what she liked with them – sell them or give them to the poor. Florence was banished from her own home and had nowhere to go. Not long after, Lee McGregor sold *Vaalbos Knop*.

> *My father did not tell Davy that he had put the farm up for sale.*
> *It was a huge farm and was split into eight separate farms to be sold.*
> *Davy had expected to inherit it one day and his sorrow and anger were immense. He had worked to build it up and was passionate about his cattle. He was furious with his father and did not speak to him for some years. Mother kept encouraging him to contact his father. After his first child was born he eventually did so, saying, "Come and see your grandchild." Father went to the farm to see Davy, his wife Pleasant, and the child.*

Davy was forced to support himself for the first time in his life. He found work with Ward Gant as manager of his farm *Sydney-on-Vaal*. Florence moved with him and his family, to live in a small room at the back of the manager's house. She was grateful that her son had arranged this.

LEE MCGREGOR was a man of formality and reserve and was almost certainly aware that his relationship with Agnes was socially awkward. Johannesburg in those days was a small, conservative society. For a man to replace a wife in his home with a mistress was unacceptable to many. People talked. Gossip had it that a great surgeon had ruined his life with "some woman". A certain doctor who had often worked with McGregor, cut him dead on the golf course.

> *Going to his rooms early, on one occasion, I saw him, through the open door, sitting with his head in his hands, and the saddest look on his face. After Agnes moved into our home, my father developed terrible migraine headaches, which troubled him for the rest of his life. He gave up everything for Agnes – respectability, social acceptance, his career, his wife... they saw nobody, and nobody was invited to see them.*

Surgeon, author, teacher, pioneer in new surgical techniques, Lee McGregor chose to retire in 1954. He was 60 and had served the Johannesburg Hospital and the Witwatersrand University Medical School for over 30 years. In due course the Johannesburg house was sold, and before moving to Somerset West near Cape Town, he and Agnes moved to a flat in town.

In 1956 Sandra's father made it clear to her that she could not go back to Florence, but should go straight to London, to live and paint there. Presumably he no longer had the excess funds for her luxurious life-style in Florence, and thought London life would be more economical. Sandra did not dare contradict her father for she still relied on him for everything. She did as she was told.

Before Sandra left for London, Agnes told her bluntly that her father had looked after her all her life, and at the age of twenty-eight it was time she earned her own living. Sandra had no idea what this entailed. She had never given money any serious thought. She had sold a few paintings, but for practically nothing. In Agnes's opinion Sandra was spoilt and self-centred, and much too demanding of her father.

AFTER THE STRESSFUL EVENTS in Johannesburg, Sandra's sudden departure from Italy and return to London after five years in Florence was a disorienting change.

She found a place to live and a real studio in which to work. The studio was in Moravian Close near the Chelsea embankment. It was on the property of Mary Gillick, a famous sculptor, who in open competition had won the design for a portrait of the Queen's head on coinage. The entrance, at 381 King's Road, led to Mary Gillick's house and three studios set in a beautiful garden. Each studio was in a separate cottage on ground level. Mary Gillick used one, Dorothy Colles, an artist renowned for her portraits of children, was installed in the second, and with Wynne-Thomas from Heatherley's, Sandra went to look at the third. They found it delightful and Sandra took it.

It was large with a skylight window, perfect for portraiture, and an artist's 'throne' – a platform big enough to have a chair on it, to enable the artist to look up at the model, and so give the portrait more dignity. A large cupboard had shelves for canvases and space on top for paints and brushes, and there was a sink on one side. In the middle of the room were a big table and sofa, and an anthracite stove in one corner kept the studio warm.

Sandra found lodging with a former acquaintance and friend of her father's, Dr. EP Scott, and his wife Marjory, in their house in Portland Place. However, wanting fewer restrictions and more independence, she soon moved to a block of flats in Hallam Street. Later she moved to the White House, not far from Regent's Park, which had the convenience of a porter, cleaners, chemist, grocer, and other shops on the ground floor. She settled there for the next three years, until 1961.

SANDRA SUBMITTED three portraits, *Maria Gloria*, *Himu* and *Mrs Holmes*, to the Royal Society of Portrait Painters in London. All three were accepted. The portraits of Maria Gloria and Himu, painted in Italy, were among the few paintings Sandra brought from Italy to England, and later to South Africa. Mrs Holmes, the elegant mother of an art school friend, Brenda, was painted in the Chelsea studio. She sat for Sandra wearing a smart dress with a boa around her shoulders. Of the three portraits *Maria Gloria* is the only one on record. The whereabouts of the other two are unknown.

Founded in 1891, this distinguished society was devoted to the art and development of portrait painting. To ensure that it would be in 'the foremost rank of art societies of the day', the premier portraitists of the time, Millais, Watts and Whistler, were soon elected to membership. The society grew, adding eminent portrait painters over the years. Women were admitted from the start. The Society promoted excellence in portrait painting in all its forms, regardless of style or popularity, and held annual exhibitions which attracted the cognoscenti of the art world and high society. To be exhibited there was for Sandra gratifying recognition of her work.

This is what Lee McGregor envisaged for his daughter – fame and recognition as a great portrait painter. Sandra's recognition from the Royal

Sandra McGregor – 'Onse artist' in District Six

Portrait of Maria Gloria
circa 1954/5
73 x 59cm
Oil on canvas
Signed bottom right

PRIVATE COLLECTION

I painted this portrait of Maria Gloria, Primo Conti's 17 year-old daughter, in her father's studio in Fiesole. Maria reluctantly sat in for an absent model one day – hence her somewhat disgruntled look.

Society of Portrait Painters was most acceptable to him. On one of his trips to England, he showed his delight at this achievement by celebrating with Sandra 'in royal manner' at the Savoy. She danced proudly with her father once again. He bought her a beautiful ermine stole from a furrier in Park Lane, and had her name embroidered on the small pocket inside.

SANDRA NOW WANTED to focus on portrait painting. She had studied Rembrandt all her life and felt that no other artist ever used the drama of light and dark as well as he did. Rembrandt's studio in the poor quarter of Amsterdam was panelled and small high windows admitted little light. He did not use artificial lighting, nor did he use candlelight to achieve his chiaroscuro. Many of Rembrandt's greatest portraits were of tramps and beggars whom he found in the Jewish quarter of Amsterdam. Although he dressed his models in interesting clothing, Sandra felt that Rembrandt, more than any other artist, painted the heart and soul of his sitters.

Sandra bought old clothes in which her models could pose on the big 'throne' in the studio: among them a green coat with a fur collar, and a soft, dark green velvet cloak, with an inner lining of red satin. She set about some serious painting. Various people in London bought Sandra's portraits, and she remembers in particular a smart South African woman, Mrs Tullis, who lived in London with her son John, who worked with Norman Hartnell, Dressmaker to the Queen. She wore one of John's creations for the sitting. Stella Jaeger, who used to invite Sandra for weekends, and another South African, 'Skattie' Boulting, who was a leading fashion model for *Vogue*, also sat for Sandra.

It was in this studio that Sandra painted a portrait of her mother wearing a black and gold shawl, *La Madre*, and drew portraits of Florence and her brother, Davy, using Hardtmuth Austrian pencils. Hardtmuth pencils were unobtainable in London but Sandra had brought boxes of them from Rigacci in Italy

Sandra produced another painting in which Florence, looking unhappy, is wearing her own Persian lamb coat. This portrait was given to Davy who no longer knows its whereabouts, and there is no record of it.

Florence had come to live in the White House in London to be close to her daughter and help her where she could. She stayed there for three years until ill health obliged her to return to South Africa, to live once again with Davy and his family. Sandra and her mother had separate flats in the White House, each with its own small kitchen. Florence shopped and cooked for Sandra, searching for food her daughter would like and shopping at a

Drawing of Florence in London
1956
39 x 29cm
Hardtmuth Austrian pencil on paper
Signed bottom right

SANDRA McGREGOR

Things fall apart

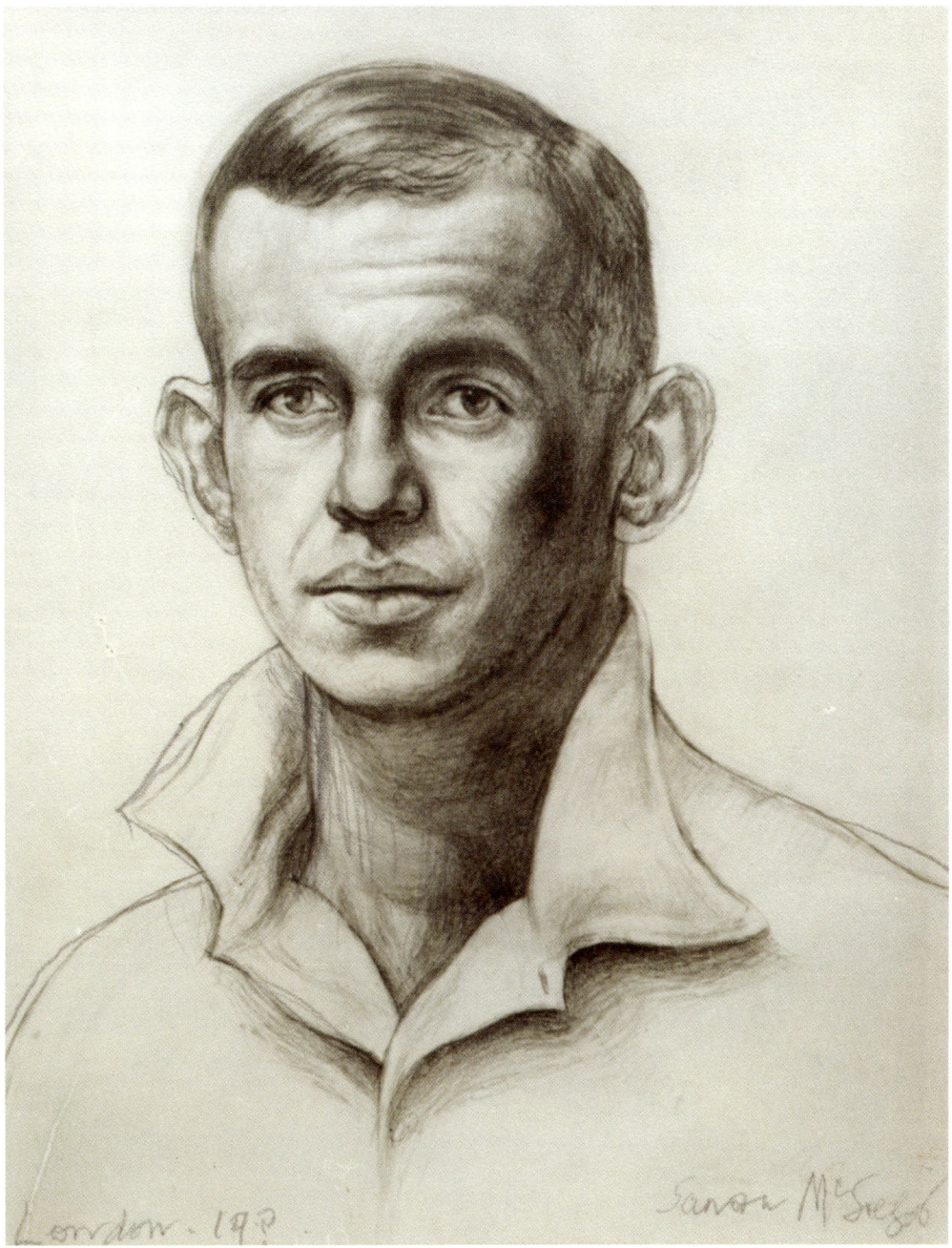

Drawing of Sandra's brother, Davy, in London

1958
51 x 41cm
Hardtmuth Austrian pencil
Signed bottom right

PRIVATE COLLECTION

I made this drawing of Davy in my Chelsea studio when he came to London to visit me and my mother.
Hardtmuth Austrian pencils were ideal for fine drawing with the lead of such good quality that the finished drawing had the feeling and texture of an etching.

Sandra McGregor – 'Onse artist' in District Six

LEFT

La Madre – Portrait of Florence McGregor with gold and black shawl
circa 1957
50 x 40cm
Oil on board
Signed bottom right

SANDRA McGREGOR

This is a tragic portrait of my mother which I exhibited in Cape Town at my first exhibition at the Regency Art Gallery in 1963 and again at the Baxter Theatre in 1990.

nearby market for fresh fruit and vegetables. Sometimes they went out together, occasionally to see a film. Their communication however was mainly at night when Sandra went to Florence for the evening meal.

Florence must have received financial support or a settlement from Lee McGregor who legally was still her husband. She never granted him the divorce he asked for. Sandra's parents were married in community of property, but she does not know any settlement details as they never discussed such matters.

ALTHOUGH SHE WAS NOT HIS WIFE, Lee McGregor arranged a 'honeymoon' for Agnes, who had never been out of South Africa.

I was told to book a suite for them at Grosvenor House in Park Lane, and I did so in the names of Mr. Lee McGregor and Miss A. Stevenson. Agnes was furious. My father just shrugged his shoulders. She had arrived, clutching onto his arm, taller than he was, on those dreadful high heels she always wore. I noticed the beautiful diamond earrings that he had given her, before she left the Lady Dudley Nursing Home. She could have found no better way of proclaiming her power over my father.

Sandra's father took Agnes shopping at Harrods where in the clothing departments her figure was much admired. He showed her the sights of London and had arranged to take her to Scotland, Paris and Italy. Tactlessly, he asked Sandra if she would like to accompany them – evidently oblivious of Sandra's dislike of Agnes.

Much as I loved my father I could not face even the thought of how she would behave. She took over completely, clutching my father's left arm and willing that I should not be able to converse with my father – I could not get a word out. I still believe that as a nurse she knew something of hypnosis – she certainly practised it on me.

When Sandra's father and Agnes returned from touring, Sandra had more finished work to show her father, who visited her in the studio in Chelsea. She was at this time painting portraits of Londoners from all walks of life, such as Mr. Alexiou, a Cypriot restaurant owner, Paul Asiack, an opera singer and Alan Battenberg, a London lawyer.

Before Lee and Agnes left for South Africa, Sandra wanted to play them some of her records, including Danny Boy, a song her father loved. Whenever they used to listen to music Sandra always sat beside him and he always held her hand.

I was on his right, Agnes on his left, and he held both of our hands, which was ridiculous.

My mother was in London when Lee and Agnes came to England. She would stand outside Grosvenor House, hoping to catch sight of the husband she still yearned for.

SANDRA WAS SOON CAUGHT UP in London life again and gave a party in her Chelsea studio to introduce her friends to Pietro Annigoni. Florence helped cater for the occasion and musicians were engaged. Sandra was delighted when Annigoni admired some of her own portraits.

The party was a great success. Music and dancing went on until the musicians, pre-booked by Sir Archibald Macindoe a colleague of my father, had to leave. I called my mother after midnight from a public phone and asked her to come and help clean up the studio. She came by taxi and we worked together until the early hours.

THE STRESS SANDRA SUFFERED at seeing her father with Agnes, may well have triggered her long battle with bulimia which started one evening in London after dinner with a friend.

She had been given a large box of chocolates and, although for years she had resisted, she ate one and then quickly finished the entire box. In shock but without hesitation, she put her finger down her throat and vomited. From then onward she struggled with this compulsion in secret, gorging herself and then throwing-up. From that night in London she led an appalling secret life.

I could not eat one slice of cake – I had to eat the whole cake. I could not eat one sandwich – I had to eat the entire loaf. I would cut up an entire cottage loaf, and cover each slice with butter and peanut butter. I would then open boxes of small cakes which had been delivered to my flat during the day from an Italian patisserie. I would begin with milky coffee, eat my way through the sandwiches, and then start on the cakes – rum-babas, lemon curd tartlets, strawberry shortbread, chocolate cakes and marzipan cakes all iced, sugary or filled with thick cream. I told curious friends the cake deliveries were for parties, and no one was aware of what was happening. I thanked God that neither of my parents knew.

Portrait of Mr Alexiou, a Cypriot restaurant owner
Late 1950s
60 x 51cm
Oil on Sundela Panel
Signed bottom right

PRIVATE COLLECTION

Mr Alexiou owned a fashionable Chelsea restaurant in the King's Road where we would sometimes dine. He arrived for the sitting wearing an old macintosh which suited my dark Rembrandt palette perfectly.

Sundela panels consisted of layers of pressed wood which had to be primed but gave a smooth painting surface.

I met Paul Asiack at Covent Garden. Half Italian, half Maltese, he had a marvellous, smouldering expression and willingly agreed to sit for me.

Portrait of Paul Asiack, an opera singer
Late 1950s
60 x 51cm
Oil on canvas
Signature bottom right trimmed.

PRIVATE COLLECTION

Things fall apart

Portrait of Alan Battenberg, a London lawyer
late 1950s
60 x 51cm
Oil on canvas
Signature bottom right trimmed.

PRIVATE COLLECTION

Sandra would paint all day, only waiting for six o'clock to put down her brushes, then lay into an enormous amount of food. She would sometimes have dinner with her mother, bid her goodnight and hasten to her flat for another binge.

She continued to draw and paint in her studio, but the driving force in her life became eating, not painting.

◆

CHAPTER 6

Apprenticeship

Mrs Gillick, Sandra's neighbour in the grounds of the Chelsea studio, had become a friend and introduced her to Douglas Bisset, a fine draftsman and renowned Scottish sculptor. After Sandra showed him her work, he pulled a pencil stub out of his pocket and produced a rapid drawing of a Greek figure. Sandra realised she could learn from his remarkable way of drawing. At her request, Florence, who was still living in London, arranged for her to study with Bisset in Glasgow.

Douglas Bisset had a brilliant mind and was extraordinarily well read. He had served an apprenticeship as a stone carver, while attending classes at the Glasgow School of Art. Winning the Keppie Scholarship in 1932, he travelled to Copenhagen for further study under the Danish neo-classical sculptor Aksel (Axel) Utzon-Frank, a former pupil of the French artist, Aristide Maillol.

Utzon-Frank laid emphasis on solid craftsmanship skills. He was a teacher of great importance and came to dominate several generations of sculptors, including Henry Heerup, Janus Kamban, and Douglas Bisset.

Bisset later won the Prix de Rome, which enabled him to tour Italy and Greece, where he worked in Athens for the British School of Archeology. He returned to Britain and became Head of Sculpture at Leeds School of Art and the City and Guilds School of Art in London. He received commissions for architectural sculpture and later specialised in private commissions of bronze busts and nude figures.

IN HIS OWN TEACHING, BISSET often quoted artists and philosophers to inspire his students. The following excerpt comes from a letter written by Emile Zola to his great friend the artist Paul Cezanne, who was unable to sell any work and was impoverished.

In the artist there are two men – the artist and the workman.
One is born an artist, one becomes a workman. And you who have the spark, who possess what cannot be acquired, you complain, when all you need do to succeed, is to exercise your fingers – to become a workman. **EMILE ZOLA**

Sandra recalls Bisset quoting philosophers too.

A part can only be rendered in art by a knowledge of the whole. **ARISTOTLE**.

Perhaps Douglas Bisset's most important words for Sandra were,

> *The unity is the chief thing in a work of art, and the part shall subserve the whole.* DOUGLAS BISSET

Sandra acknowledges indebtedness to Douglas Bisset for all she knows of Monumental Art and three dimensional drawing. Monumental Art aspires to convey the grand and noble, and relates to timelessness in architecture, such as the pyramids or large friezes: it is not a synonym for 'large'. In 1957, Bisset wrote, 'On seeing the Acropolis you will cry. It is not an emotion with the ground long prepared for tears, but an overwhelming power that wrings tears from your reasoning.' This describes his interpretation of Monumental Art.

Sandra applied this concept of Monumental Art to her drawing in which the three dimensions of objects are perceived – as one would a sculpture in reality – in the round. This is achieved by shading and tone in drawing, and requires real skill: vision, understanding of light and form, discipline, and perseverance as well as an ability to draw. It was this approach, this Form – making the image project from the page – which made an impact on Sandra.

Her time in Scotland, studying with Douglas Bisset, was a definitive year in Sandra's apprenticeship. Douglas was years older than Sandra, but with him and his friends Sandra went frequently to Helensburgh on weekends, visited the exquisite island of Iona, enjoyed long walks, and spent hours talking and discussing art. He changed her whole attitude to drawing by opening her eyes and enabling her to see. She had never met anyone who could draw and sculpt as he could.

> *He was the greatest draughtsman I ever met and was so fine a teacher that (later) I was able to hand on to my students much of what he taught me.*

Douglas Bisset inspired Sandra, gave her new life, and she returned to London brimming with enthusiasm and ideas.

She had no parental visits in Glasgow, neither did she have time nor inclination to visit Edinburgh to meet her half-sisters.

SHE PRACTISED HER new approach to drawing diligently. Simultaneously this made Sandra review the way she had been taught to paint: she wanted to learn the techniques of the Old Masters. A bookseller at Zwemmers, a prominent bookshop in Charing Cross Road, told her that there was but one expert who could teach this: Helmut Ruhemann, the leading restorer at the

National Gallery, who at that time was teaching in America. Ruhemann's book on the subject *The Artist at Work*, was out of print but fortunately the bookseller located a second-hand copy which Sandra purchased.

Meanwhile, Sandra had met Paul Harmann, a German who had a studio in St. John's Wood. He was Jewish and well known in Hamburg as an excellent sculptor. He fled to Paris from the Nazis thinking he would be safe there, but after France's surrender, moved to London where he began teaching. Many of his students were Jewish, and sometimes Sandra would join the class. Sandra became friends with Harmann and his wife Paula, and on one occasion Paula asked Sandra to pose for Paul's students. Sandra immediately said, "No". However, when Paula asked her to take off her clothes and stand in a natural position, Sandra agreed. The Harmanns both declared that she would be a good model, and in due course she posed for Harmann's adult sculpture classes and was paid a token amount. Sandra's mother was appalled.

Upon Ruhemann's return from the United States, Sandra studied with him in London for three months. She discovered that following political changes in 1933, Helmut Ruhemann had also left Germany for England. He settled in London, and made his living as an art restorer. He himself was an artist, but felt that his living would be more secure in restoration work. He became one of the leading picture restorers of his generation, and from 1934 restored paintings for the National Gallery and later for the Glasgow Art Gallery. He was appointed consultant restorer at the National Gallery in 1946 and held this post when Sandra met him. He also lectured at the Courtauld Institute of Art from 1934.

During her studies with Ruhemann, Sandra wrote down much of what he told her, and referred to his books when she painted. He motivated and inspired her, giving her a solid foundation for all her future painting.

… begin by 'drawing-in' using pencil or charcoal. Then go over this drawing with blue oil paint; model with the paint. But don't lay in dark shadows. Shadows must always be thin and transparent. Lights thin and opaque. Paint vividly and spontaneously, modelling with your brush. Remember that lights will not tell on white, so the darker and stronger the half-tone beneath them, the more they will vibrate.

Beauty of colour lies not in its strength, but in its clarity and precision. Go for precision and variegation, that is changing from one colour to another, which makes it interesting and rich. The great secret lies in half-tones…

> *To make your highlights tell, lay in a general yellow tone, raw sienna for example (over your fixed pencil or charcoal drawing).*
>
> *If you lose the half-tones you will stop the form going round – this is the basis of Monumental drawing and painting.* **HELMUT RUHEMANN**

In later years, Sandra passed on much of her own extensive knowledge and experience to her own pupils. She can still quote by heart the lines which the Greek writer Pliny wrote of Parrhasios, the famous 5th century BC Greek painter. In Europe after the Renaissance, Parrhasios' name became synonymous with excellence.

> *By the admission of artists he was supreme in contour. This is the last subtlety of painting, in which many have been famous, but to paint the disappearing planes is rare in the history of art. For the contour must go round itself and so end, that it promises other things behind and shows that which it hides.* **PLINY**

Helmut Ruhemann changed Sandra's style and she never departed from the principles he taught her, abandoning the traditional style of her early paintings.

EVENTUALLY SANDRA was obliged to leave the Chelsea studio as it was too expensive. She found another studio in St John's Wood, near Portland Place. Sandra still had little idea of the costs she was incurring, but she began to work hard again. Finally, she gave up both the St John's Wood studio and the White House, moving into a flat on the top floor of a big house in Gloucester Place where there was accommodation with a studio above, leading to the rooftop. Her mother remained living in the White House until she returned to South Africa.

While Sandra was living in Gloucester Place, she had the most joyful and subsequently saddest love affair of her life. In a chance encounter she met Major General Jack Benoit, a retired British Army officer. He was much older than Sandra – 68 to her 30 years – and resembled her father in appearance. He told her he was separated from his wife who lived in the country and that he had two adopted children. He never spoke about his wife and Sandra never met the children.

Jack was at that time involved in the Design Centre at 28 Haymarket, near Piccadilly Circus. The Centre was opened by Prince Philip, the Duke of Edinburgh, in 1956, to provide a permanent public space in which to present a standing display of contemporary British design and changing programmes of themed special exhibitions.

Jack was also interested in art and well known in art circles. For the first time in her life, Sandra fell deeply in love. She became obsessed with Jack. and stopped painting altogether. She found Jack attractive sexually and all she wanted was to spend the rest of her life with him. For some years they did everything together. They went to restaurants, theatres, films, danced, and travelled on weekends, thoroughly enjoying each other's company. Sandra did not tell her father. She would never have dared, but her mother knew. Florence met Jack only once and did not frequent Sandra's Gloucester Road flat.

Ultimately, some of Sandra's friends, realising that the relationship had no future, urged her to return to South Africa. A spiritualist, Lilian Bailey, whom Sandra and her mother consulted occasionally, warned that Jack was still married and that his relationship with Sandra was just another affair to him. Lilian's daughter, Dorothy, a sophisticated editor of a woman's magazine, advised Sandra to leave Jack. She could see that Jack had no intention of marrying Sandra and urged her to leave him, to return to South Africa. Sandra resisted their advice for as long as possible

Mrs MacLeod, an elderly and concerned friend of Sandra's, perturbed by Sandra's obvious unhappiness, asked what was the matter. Sandra told her that she wanted to marry Jack, but that he had never asked her. Mrs MacLeod replied, "If he hasn't asked you, he doesn't want to marry you." She told Sandra to hand matters over to God who would give her the courage to leave.

Sandra did not have the courage. She felt as her father felt about Agnes – felt she could not possibly live without Jack. She was too distressed to see the situation clearly, and did not see what others saw.

She did not realise then that in Jack she had found a father figure whom she could love in every way. Only much later when she underwent Jungian analysis did she accept her love for Jack as a replacement for her oedipal longing for her father. It was her father she had been in love with, not Jack. Then she also understood how her father's infatuation with Agnes dominated his life, how he ultimately used his funds for his mistress rather than his daughter, and how his own daughter had to accept second place.

AT THE SAME TIME as Sandra was being urged to leave by her friends, her father must have realised that she was not painting. He wrote and made it clear that he was no longer prepared to maintain her financially, that she should come back to South Africa and earn her own living. It seemed to Sandra that her beloved father was willing to reject her to please Agnes.

Sandra had never earned her own living, and certainly had no conception of what it meant to do so. Money was something that came regularly from her father. She would never have thought of getting work in London to enable her to stay on. Sandra's father still came first. She could not disobey him, and even at thirty-four, and despite her love for Jack, she was emotionally still deeply dependent on her father. She had no option but to leave.

Sandra went to the bank and was appalled to find how little money was in her account. She had just enough left to buy a ticket home. On the day she left Jack put her into a taxi for the airport. His last words were, "Goodbye darling, good luck! I'll be waiting for you when you come back." Sandra sobbed all the way to the airport and intermittently on the long flight to South Africa. In her desperate unhappiness she could not speak to anyone on the plane.

Jack did not know that Sandra had no home to go to, nor did he suspect that she was going for good. Sandra never returned to England. Much later she tore up two drawings she had done of him.

SANDRA HAD BEEN LIVING IN EUROPE for sixteen years, of which the last six had been spent in Britain. In all these years she had never owned a home of her own, moving from lodging to lodging; never driven a car, relying on taxis, friends or public transport; forming relationships with many unsuitable men, none of which lasted. Now she was being torn from the one she wanted to keep, perhaps the most unsuitable of all.

In these sixteen years she had been given an extensive art education, lived in some of Europe's greatest cities, learnt a lot, but had little to show for it, bar a few paintings. Had her considerable talent been squandered through over-indulgence from her parents? Had it resulted in a complete lack of motivation and the will to succeed? She appeared to lack any desire to succeed, or support herself. In spite of this privileged upbringing, at thirty-four and still very attractive, her future was uncertain.

Sandra left London in the summer, for home in South Africa where it was winter. But where was home? She was not welcome in Somerset West where her father was living with Agnes. Her mother, who had recently returned to South Africa, was living on the Ward Gant farm near Kimberley, with Davy and his family. Sandra felt that there was no-one to care about her, or for her.

She sold her books, gave away many of her possessions, and left

Gloucester Place to fly to Johannesburg, sending only her clothes, a few paintings and some personal belongings by sea to Cape Town. By this time her allowance had been drastically cut, and finally stopped altogether. It was time for Sandra to grow up.

PART 2

CHAPTER 7

An open door in Keerom Street

Sandra returned from England in 1962, her destination Cape Town. There was nothing left for her in Johannesburg. The family home in Parktown West had been sold, the McGregor farm had long gone, as had Glencrag where they had experienced such holiday happiness, and her mother was living with Davy and family on the farm, *Sydney on Vaal*, near Kimberley. Sandra chose to make a new life in Cape Town because it was close to Somerset West and she could visit her father easily.

From Cape Town, another train took Sandra to Somerset West and on arrival Sandra rang her father from the station. She was longing to be with him again and assumed she would stay with him and Agnes in their house. To her disappointment they had booked a room for her in a small hotel in Somerset West. She realised that she would never be able to stay with her father again.

In her first days in Cape Town Sandra took a room at the Leonora Hotel, Green Point, run by a kind English woman. Florence came from Kimberley to join her, lodging at The Avalon, a boarding house nearby. In all the years of hardship that were to follow, it was Sandra's mother who helped her financially when she could. Sandra could now barely afford to live. Sad and depressed, she never wanted to paint again and had lost confidence. She was still plagued by bulimia: driven by an urge she could not control – driven to eat, not to paint.

Buck Jones, Sandra's mentor and trusted friend.

WANDERING DISCONSOLATELY down Keerom Street one day, Sandra happened to look into an open door. There was a man sitting at a desk in an office.

"Hello," he said. "Come in. Have some coffee."

These simple words, this gesture of friendship, led to Sandra's great fortune in meeting Buck Jones, a man who became her friend, her helper, her source of enthusiastic encouragement, and, above all, the one person who restored her faith in herself. Sandra had lost all desire to paint, but Buck persuaded her to start painting again and consequently opened a new life for her to express herself.

He immediately realised that a place to work was essential for Sandra's well-being. He found accommodation for her at the bottom of Kloof Street, not far from the Long Street Baths. Jack Kaltenbrum, a fine sculptor, and his

Hanover Building, District Six, Cape Town, 1962.

wife Pat, owned a double-storey house where many artists had lived. There was a large, sunny studio, a little bedroom, and a scullery with a sink and cold running water, on the top floor – no bathroom, but an outside shower under a grape vine and a toilet in the garden.

Buck helped Sandra move, found some curtains and set up the studio for her. Florence stayed on in Green Point and still did whatever she could for Sandra. When Sandra needed a chair for her room, it was her mother who took her to a second-hand shop off Long Street to buy one, and paid R25 for it.

Buck took her to the docks to fetch the boxes from London which contained her possessions, including her art equipment. He later made a wardrobe for her using these boxes.

"Now start painting," he said.

"I don't know what to paint."

"Paint the chair. If you don't start I will never come back."

Sandra's relationship with Buck was vital in those early years in Cape Town, when everything seemed to have crashed around her. Buck, a man of forty-five, was a photographer, working for an Afrikaans magazine called *Ster*. He was creative and talented and longed to become a full-time sculptor. He achieved this later, with the help of Lippy Lipschitz, creating beautiful sculptures in wood. Buck appreciated all art forms and believed in Sandra's potential. He also came to understand her deep unhappiness.

SANDRA STARTED PAINTING AGAIN. *Buck's Chair* was the first oil painting to be produced in her Kloof Street studio. She had brought paints back from England and her Italian palette from Rigacci, the famous art shop in Florence. Buck came regularly from his office to see how she was getting on, and the chair became the painting of a friendship. It took two weeks to complete.
Buck Jones was full of enthusiasm, love of life, people, nature, the sea – he loved everything beautiful. She worked at her best because of Buck, just as she had worked to do well for her father at school. She had been so unhappy leaving England, but with Jack and Pat Kaltenbrum in this warm lively house, full of sunshine, she regained her *joie de vivre*.

BUCK CAME TO UNDERSTAND Sandra very well. Although she was careful to hide her addiction and was confident that nobody knew her secret, Buck, himself a former alcoholic, was suspicious of her behaviour. Once again he tried to help her. He introduced her to open meetings of Alcoholics

Buck's Chair
1962
110 x 50cm
Panel – oil on board
Signed bottom right on shadow of chair leg

PRIVATE COLLECTION

Buck's Chair *is a special painting for me as it brings back so many memories and feelings: the chair was a gift from my mother and the table from my new landlord, Jack Kaltenbrum; the books which Buck and I read together –* Kahlil Gibran's The Prophet, *was a favourite; the green ashtray Buck always used was made for me by Paula Harmann, a potter and friend in London; and the door knob which for me represents the opening of a new door – a new life.*

Indian art has always fascinated me and the small drawing of an Indian figure represents the many hours I spent in the Victoria and Albert Museum in London sketching and drawing Indian art. The Pisces fish was Buck's birth sign.

Florence in Greenpoint, Cape Town
1962
59 x 46cm
Sepia ink and gouache on yellow-ochre paper
Signed in black ink on spine of book.

SANDRA McGREGOR

I made this drawing of my mother, Florence, in the boarding house in Green Point, where she was staying at this time. It was cold and my mother was wearing her winter coat. I drew her sitting on her bed.

We seldom met, however, and she only met Buck once. She was unhappy in Cape Town and complained that money was short. She asked Davy to take her back to the farm. Years later, when I was teaching at the Technical College, I occasionally went by train, in the holidays, to visit her.

RIGHT
At Buck's suggestion I painted two panels in oil of rooftops in the Malay Quarter, as seen from my studio window. The different planes of the roof surfaces in sunlight and shade gave me a compositional and colour challenge.

An open door in Keerom Street

Malay Quarter rooftops in sunlight
1962/63
110 x 50cm
Panel – oil on board
No visible signature

OWNER UNKNOWN

Reproduced from a photographic print

Malay Quarter rooftops as the sun is setting
1962/63
110 x 50cm
Panel – oil on board
No visible signature

PRIVATE COLLECTION

Malay Quarter rooftops
1962/63
75 x 54cm
Pen, ink and gouache
Signed bottom left

RIGHT REVEREND JAMES PATRICK

I exhibited Malay Quarter rooftops *at my first solo exhibition at the Regency Gallery, Cape Town in 1963.*

An open door in Keerom Street

The Black Trunk
1962/63
110 x 50cm
Panel – oil on board
No visible signature

DISTRICT SIX MUSEUM

Reproduced from a photographic print

My father brought this trunk back from a visit to America, as a gift when I was a young girl. It was filled with beautiful clothes for me and an excellent shooting rifle for Davy. I travelled extensively with this theatrical black trunk, with its 'tray' on top and much space underneath, and used it to store things for many years.

Sandra McGregor – 'Onse artist' in District Six

Sandra's Kloof Street studio
1962/63
110 x 50cm
Panel – oil on board
Signed bottom right

OWNER UNKNOWN

My flat in Kloof Street was small but bright. I painted my studio from my bedroom – almost a painting within a painting

An open door in Keerom Street

Lantern with red background
1963/64
60 x 50cm
Oil on board
Signed top right

PRIVATE COLLECTION

Sandra McGregor – 'Onse artist' in District Six

Lantern with yellow duster
1963/64
60 x 50cm
Oil on board
Signed bottom right

MALINDA DU RANDT

The lantern in this painting – and that on Page 67 – belonged to Buck. He suggested I include the yellow duster because it 'lit' the lamp.

Anonymous (AA), where she met people with addictions, heard their stories, and listened to speakers. She came to understand that her favourite foods were as damaging to her as alcohol was to others. She did not divulge her problem, but felt at home there, and frequently went to the weekly meetings. Buck did not accompany her.

Over the years, Buck continued to protect and encourage Sandra. They became very fond of one another, and their interest in art bonded them deeply. She did not love Buck as she had Jack, and their relationship did not develop into an affair. Buck was a married man. Sandra knew his wife and his sister Lettie, and met some of their other relatives, all of whom became friends.

After several years, Buck was transferred to Durban, and moved there with his family. Sandra spoke to him once or twice, but never saw him again. Sadly he died some years ago of cancer, but Sandra has never forgotten him, nor her debt of gratitude. She still treasures her photograph of him, and her painting of *Buck's Chair*, which hangs in her room.

IN THE WINTER OF 1962 when Buck was certain that Sandra was more settled and happy to be painting again, he took her to District Six. Little did she know how this introduction would change her life.

On that very first visit she saw immediately, with joy, the possibilities that existed for painting: the life, the people, the buildings, the spirit of the District caught her imagination, and a strange excitement welled up in her.

I felt something tremendous move inside me and immediately knew
this was where I had to paint.

CHAPTER 8

Motjie Ragmat's kitchen

Portrait of Juleiga
1963/64
74 x 48cm
Cray-pas on strawboard
Signed bottom left

JULIAN ADLER

I found the Cape Malays enchanting people to draw and paint, and knew Motjie Ragmat's granddaughter, Juleiga, would make a beguiling subject with her striking brown eyes.
I chose cray-pas on strawboard with its a coarse texture, to provide a good base for Juleiga's golden skin. A fall as a small child had resulted in a slightly skew jaw which was corrected later in life.
I painted this portrait in Motjie Ragmat's house over three to four days. Juleiga patiently sat for about four hours at a time.
I gave this portrait as a gift to Julian Adler's wife, Joyce, who was a close friend. They both took a great interest in my work, and Julian sold many of my paintings for me.

B*uck's Chair* marks the start of a remarkable eighteen years, 1962-1979, that Sandra spent painting in District Six. Her studies with Helmut Ruhemann and Douglas Bisset led to a radical change of style, and rejection of the earlier more formal methods she had been taught. Sandra drew and painted scene after scene, person after person, indoors and outdoors. These works are a progressive record of the life of a society and heritage which was ultimately destroyed before her eyes.

District Six was situated on the lower slopes of Devil's Peak at the east end of the city of Cape Town. It developed in Victorian times into a largely working-class area of steep cobbled streets, alleyways and lanes, with single and double-storey houses and buildings, shops, churches and mosques. Development accelerated in the late 19th century when people from all over the world were attracted to southern Africa by the discoveries of diamonds and gold. In the early 20th century, immigrants from Europe predominated and many settled in Cape Town where, as their first port of call, they could find work.

By the mid 20th century, as racial legislation intensified, the inhabitants of District Six were mostly coloured working-class people. Close to the Castle, the Grand Parade and the City Hall, and within walking distance of the docks, District Six became a symbol of Capetonian urban coloured identity, and produced professional and public figures who lived side by side amongst the working-class inhabitants.

In 1966 the apartheid government declared District Six an area set aside for white occupation only. Then began the protest marches, the anger and frustration. Soon the bulldozers began their punitive work. Many people left before the major demolitions started. Others waited until told to go. Finally, the entire community was removed to designated out-lying areas on the windswept Cape Flats, such as Mitchell's Plain, Hanover Park, Lentegeur, Grassy Park, Bonteheuwel, and Manenberg.

This is the District Six that Sandra came to know, express and record without restraint.

SANDRA'S WORK was ahead of its time in South Africa. There was little demand for such intimate and sensitive depictions of District Six and its people's way of life, nor for Sandra's bold and colourful brush strokes.

What Sandra discovered was a community of people who welcomed her kindness, generosity, and humanity and took her into their hearts and homes. The local working-class people became her most enthusiastic if impecunious fans. To have their largely misunderstood and sometimes feared world recorded by a friendly, professional white artist who was interested in them and their surroundings, intrigued and delighted them.

Sandra became well-known in the District and the friends she made there remained loyal to her long after the District was demolished. She was never molested by any of the rogues or gangs and was one of few whites – let alone a white woman – who ventured there regularly. Her whole purpose in life was to paint in District Six.

She was often seen sitting painting, in the streets or amongst the rubble, surrounded by children, recording real people for posterity. Like many artists, she sold her canvases for a few rands almost as soon as the paint on them was dry, keeping no records of who had bought them. The concept of earning a living still remained foreign to her. Known as 'Miss Sand-er-a' she was welcomed by all, including the most hardened 'skollies'.

There was nothing gradual about Sandra's introduction to District Six.

Sandra painting in District Six.

Lonely desperation dissolved and a new passion seized her from the moment Buck took her there.

> *Hanover Street on lovely summer's day. Buck drove to Hanover Street, to the Seven Steps. Got out of the combi and he pointed to the Seven Steps and the steps to Caledon Street at the other end.*
>
> *Most strange – not a soul to be seen except for a man reclining on the steps. Grey suit – long coat – one hand hidden in his pocket. He didn't say a word – I saw his incredibly green eyes. "Mr. Green Eyes".*
>
> *Buck had come with his camera – not wise; white men with cameras not welcome.*
>
> *A pink convertible hid the house. Children shout, "It belongs to Cass." I meet Cass and his boyfriend, and later his parents Ishmail and Mareldia.*
>
> *I look up the steps. I am deeply moved. I know this is where I must paint.*
>
> *Return next day alone with my art equipment. The Seven Steps swarming with people. Learnt later of people hiding behind curtains who had been watching me the day before.*
>
> *Cass suggests I take my art equipment next door. I meet my beloved Motjie Ragmat Karriem. She clears a corner in her kitchen for my boards and easel, brushes and paints. She becomes my great friend, my 'mother'.*
>
> *She tells me that the figure reclining on the steps – he was there again – was Ou Vyf – gang leader of many 'skollies' in District Six. I greet him and he is very friendly. I call him "Mr. Green Eyes" from then on – to his great amusement. He had been the renowned head of the Globe Gang in the 1920s.*
>
> *Go up Caledon Street, Hanover Street and do some quick sketching. Find marvellous scenes to paint.*
>
> *Later Buck takes me to Vernon Terrace. I ask him what shall I paint? He says, "Paint this."*

CASS GORDON, also known as Bernie, lived at the Seven Steps, near Hanover Square. His pink convertible obstructed the view of the house Sandra wanted to sketch. In answer to Sandra's knock at the front door a sleepy, half-dressed, man appeared. A lifelong friendship was to develop from this first encounter with Cass.

Sandra was to paint many portraits in this house, the home of Cass's parents Mareldia and Ishmail. Ishmail was a hawker who sold fruit and vegetables from his barrow near the central Post Office. The 'barrow-boys' as they were known, hawking fruit, vegetables and flowers, were picturesque features of Cape Town streets, with their lively banter and calls. When Sandra asked Cass if she could leave her art material in his mother's house he explained that a kind woman, Motjie Ragmat, lived next door and had more space: thus Sandra met the woman who was to become her 'mother', friend, and guardian in District Six.

Motjie Ragmat was a woman of great strength, a powerful character who was not afraid of anyone. Her good friend Ou Vyf respected her and so did the 'skollies', who admired her courage. Motjie Ragmat lived in a house at the Seven Steps where the area met Caledon Street. Once a gang leader, Ou Vyf was respected and feared. He was said to have been the fiercest fighter in District Six and had lost the fingers of one hand in a gang fight, hence his name. With these two on her side, Sandra could walk anywhere.

Motjie Ragmat cleared a whole corner of the kitchen and for nearly twenty years I kept my art equipment there. My easel and drawing boards, sketch blocks and sheets of paper, containers for my pencils and paints – gouache-paints and oils, dozens of paint brushes, my Rigacci palette. There were also blotting paper, paint rags, and palette knives.

My art equipment was not all in Motjie Ragmat's kitchen; I carried a lot with me, wherever I had chosen to work, and the children of the District carried much of it. But in all those twenty years I never lost a single thing, not even a pencil disappeared.

MOTJIE RAGMAT had been through hard times. Her husband, Abdullah, worked in the docks, loading and unloading ships. She would go out as a washerwoman, walking to the Malay Quarter, knocking on doors and fetching the clothes to wash in the big wash-house, which Sandra painted years later. Motjie Ragmat would then take them home, and later return the clothes, washed and ironed, neatly wrapped in a cloth. She always wore skirts with blouses or jerseys, under an apron of one kind or another, and covered her head with a doek.

Abdullah was a gentle and kind man. He had served as a corporal in the army during the Second World War, and later when no longer working, had only a meagre government pension. He and Motjie Ragmat brought up their children to show respect for elders, to live and dress decently, and to develop a community spirit. This spirit, this concern for others, was widely prevalent throughout the District. Sandra was close to the whole family, including the children and grandchildren.

Motjie Ragmat's children all helped in the house, laying the table, washing the dishes, the boys keeping themselves clean with cold water from a tap in the yard. Plumbing was primitive, there was no bath, no waterborne sewerage: only two 'long-drop' toilets in their yard – holes in the ground with wooden seats, and buckets which the night soil men carried away every night.

MOTJIE RAGMAT WAS A DEVOUT MUSLIM, and ultimately, after years of saving, she realised her dream of going to Mecca and becoming a Hadji. After that she was addressed as Hadji Ragmat.

I could never have managed without my dear Motjie Ragmat and her wonderful kindness. I often had supper in her home – sitting round her kitchen table – with her family, enjoying the delicious curries she used to make. When the snoek-cart came around – and we all knew the sound of the fish-horn (snoek-horn) we would enjoy the snoek, cooked in her special way.

After supper Motjie Ragmat would walk with me down Hanover Street to the Hanover Street bus stop, where I took the bus to get me to Adderley Street, from where I would walk to my flat in the Gardens. In those years it was often as late as 10 p.m. or later on lovely summer evenings.

Before they reached the bus stop they would sometimes go to the fish shop, where an old lady sold fish and chips. She would parcel the purchase in newspaper, and on freezing winter evenings it was a joy to enter her warm shop, packed with people, amid the smell of frying fish and chips. Children came for a few cents-worth of chips and they would go out into the cold, holding the hot parcel close to their chests, hoping to take a few that their mothers would not miss.

CASS GORDON GREW UP in the District and like his mother became a hairdresser. But it was not what he wanted to do: he wanted to dance. He had always been interested in drama and Spanish dancing, had a natural sense of rhythm and was creative in his dancing. Apartheid precluded different races from dancing or performing together, so sometimes he would pretend to be a dark Portuguese man.

Sandra McGregor – 'Onse artist' in District Six

Motjie Ragmat's kitchen
1962/63
110 x 50cm
Panel – oil on board
Signed bottom right

PRIVATE COLLECTION

I never painted a portrait of Motjie Ragmat, but captured her – as I often saw her – ironing in her own kitchen. The little boy in the painting, Freddie, standing in Motjie's backyard, was one of two abandoned children taken in and brought up within their family. The family grew to seven in number with Motjie Ragmat's four boys and a daughter, Aziza.

Motjie Ragmat's backyard leading to Caledon Street
early 1960s
110 x 50cm
Panel – oil on board
Signed bottom right

OWNER UNKNOWN

Motjie Ragmat's house and backyard were always filled with children, her own and others. I painted this panel showing a narrow passageway which led from Motjie's backyard into Caledon Street. Many of the people whom I painted in District Six were poor: children were mostly barefoot and toddlers without nappies or trousers.

The older girls were responsible for looking after the younger children and often carried them about. Their playgrounds were the backyards and streets.

The blue cart was just one of many such carts in the District and I painted several compositions using the cart as a central motif.

Portrait of Rashied, Motjie Ragmat's grandson.
Early 1960s
110 x 50cm
Panel – oil on board
No visible signature

OWNER UNKNOWN

Reproduced from a photographic print

I painted Rashied, one of Aziza's sons, in his traditional robes which he wore for his religious studies at the Muslim school. I often saw Rashied, charming and friendly, at his grandmother's house.

Motjie Ragmat's Kitchen

Portrait of Cass in Hadj robes
Early 1960s
110 x 50cm
Panel – oil on board
Signed top left

ROEDEAN SCHOOL (SA)

Portrait of Cass with red lantern
Early 1960s
110 x 50cm
Panel – oil on board
Signed bottom left

PRIVATE COLLECTION

Portrait of Cass
Early 1960s
110 x 500cm
Panel – oil on board
Signed top left

PRIVATE COLLECTION

This is my favourite portrait of Cass. It featured on the poster for my solo exhibition, My District Six, *at the Baxter Gallery in 1990.*

His costume was richly ornate and off-set by one beautiful drop earring. It was all so 'Indian', so rich in texture and brought with it the perfume of musk oil and joss-sticks, and the mystery of the East.

Three men, all of whom worshipped at the Cathedral, the actor Bill Curry, the writer Dennis Hatfield, and a dancer John Ramsdale, were all friends of Cass. Dennis later helped him gain admission to the University of Cape Town where he learnt classical dance, but jazz was his first love. He performed and taught in the afternoon and evening, at what became the Jazz Art and Modern Dancing School. In the morning he worked in his hairdressing salon, Maison Cass, in Hanover Street.

Cass was one of Sandra's favourite models – an elegant and natural sitter – and she painted three portraits in oil, working in his room at home which had good light. He loved wearing the colourful, rich clothes that his friends brought from the East. She also made drawings of Cass in a variety of media. Cass was a devoutly religious man who subsequently made the Hadj several times.

Cass and Sandra would drive through the streets of the District in his pink convertible, looking for men he knew who would pose for Sandra. Cass also took her to the old age home in District Six where two of the residents sat for her.

> *One, an old man called September, sat clutching a precious walking stick for three hours whilst I drew him. Another subject, Mrs Althorpe, in spite of her weariness, patiently posed in her room, her felt hat hanging behind the door, and her Bible by her bedside.*

All of this work was either sold for very little or given away. Later Cass spent five years in America, a country he loved, but unfortunately he did not have a green card and was eventually sent home.

SANDRA'S PAINTING IN DISTRICT SIX began with enormous energy and enthusiasm which never waned. She accepted that poverty, gangs, and police harassment led to violence. She witnessed some fights and their aftermath first hand, or heard about them on the street. She saw how violence affected people and tried to help where she could. Never once did this dismay her or deflect her from her purpose. Never once did anyone try to harm her. Never was she afraid.

Sandra McGregor – 'Onse artist' in District Six

CHAPTER 9

Sandra assembling work for her first solo exhibition at the Regency Gallery, Church Street, Cape Town, 1963.

'Onse artist'

Soon after Sandra started painting, she was told by the police that she must report to Caledon Square police station to apply for permission for her daily visits to District Six. Sergeant Dirk Vermeulen noted Sandra's particulars, and during the interview asked if she had any scars or birthmarks. She laughingly replied that she had only four toes on her right foot, the little toe having been removed when she was young, due to a deformity inherited from her father. He laughed too and said, "Well, I have written that down and now you have a file in Caledon Square!"

Sergeant Vermeulen was to become a good friend to Sandra. She told him about her work – drawing and painting – and he gave her advice on what she could and could not do in terms of the law.

I had been asked to judge a fancy dress competition in a house off Caledon Street. The guests would all be Muslim, so there was no alcohol to be served, only cold drinks. I asked Sergeant Vermeulen whether I could dance with my friends. No, he explained, I certainly could not do that. I could judge the competition and do some sketching – that was all.

It was a memorable experience. The costumes were dramatic in their originality and design. After the prizes had been awarded the dancing started, with much laughter. I was upset that because of the colour of my skin I could not join in.

SANDRA PAINTED DAY AFTER DAY, producing a constant body of work, developing a local reputation as an artist. A few perspicacious or appreciative people, such as Julian Adler and Miriam Potash, began to collect her work and consequently there was some press coverage. Paintings were assembled for her first solo exhibition.

The exhibition was opened on the 20 August 1963 by Dr JC Coetzee, at the Regency Gallery in Church Street. Jack Coetzee had studied in Edinburgh with Sandra's father and the two medical men knew each other well. Sandra's mother and the Kaltenbrums attended the opening: her father and Agnes came later in the week. Sandra wore her ermine stole at the opening.

Alice Friedland owned the Regency Gallery, and with her sister Ray Querido, mounted Sandra's exhibition of paintings. Among them was *The*

Sandra McGregor – 'Onse artist' in District Six

The Blue Bathroom
1963
58 x 44cm
Gouache on paper
Signed bottom left

ZENA POTASH

The walls of the bathroom were cobalt blue with a touch of French ultramarine, the bath a vivid cadmium red, the basin a bright green, and the toilet a brilliant yellow. I just had to paint this extraordinary combination.

Blue Bathroom, a painting of a brightly coloured bathroom in the house of Mrs Scholz, who lived behind a blue-green front door in Vernon Terrace. This painting was bought by Miriam Potash, for her husband David who had grown up in District Six, a place he loved. He was part of the Jewish community of the District, and came from a poor family. He went barefoot as a boy, and one of his early jobs was sweeping out the National Cinema. Later he learnt the art of making jewellery, and started his own business in a single room, eventually becoming one of the leading jewellers in Cape Town.

Sandra became friendly with David and Miriam, and she painted a portrait of their daughter, Zena, then still at school. They bought other works of Sandra's, and kept in touch for many years, inviting Sandra frequently to meals in their house in Camps Bay.

Ray Querido too, became close to Sandra. She had been allowed to pay off the expenses of an operation by Lee McGregor, and she never forgot this kindness. She became a caring and considerate friend to Sandra who often went to her home to draw and paint.

The search for paintings which had been shown on this exhibition began.

The Blue Bathroom had been taken to America by Zena Potash and her husband, when they emigrated, together with another which Zena's parents had bought, *Washline with pigeon loft*. These two paintings were traced in the most fortuitous way and eventually located in 2007 near San Francisco.

Sandra lost touch with Zena Potash. She could not remember the name of Zena's husband, and all she knew was that Zena, a psychiatrist, had lived in Washington. Without much hope of finding her, Spencer Fleischer, who lives in San Francisco, was asked to see if he could track down Zena and locate the bathroom painting – a favourite of Sandra's. Fortunately, Zena had continued to work under her maiden name and a quick Google search placed her in Walnut Creek, California. An even quicker return call from Zena to Spencer, who was in a cab in New York, confirmed that she still owned the picture. Zena's prompt email read:

> I was deeply moved to get the call from Spencer today. I have been thinking about Sandra recently, she will appreciate the synchronicity of that. Please give her my fondest love and tell her that I wish her well. I have the bathroom painting as well as its companion of a yard scene with a clothes line.
> PS I never did change my name. My husband's name is Cyrus Mancherje. Another side note is that my husband's father and my father grew up as neighbours in District Six. So the circle continues.

Mrs Scholz not only had the brightest blue bathroom, but also a 'bullet-in-the-leg' son called Leonard. Shot by the police, a bullet lodged in his thigh. Like many others in the District, Leonard was terrified of hospitals and the police, so took to his bed and remained there for weeks on end, bullet and all. Sandra came to know Mrs Scholz well.

Washline with pigeon loft
1963
58 x 45cm
Gouache on paper
Signed bottom right

ZENA POTASH

THE REGENCY GALLERY building, one of Cape Town's oldest houses, was bought from the Graaff Trust Company soon after this exhibition. The new owners intended to demolish a section which was built in 1782, to make way for a multi-storeyed complex of offices and shops. The front section, built in 1702, was to be restored and preserved. Sandra captured on canvas what she called "the historical atmosphere" of the building – a 'haunted' stairway leading from the second floor of the back portion.

Alice Friedland was saddened by the impending demolition. The lower floors will be remembered by Capetonians for the art exhibitions, auctions and events held in the showrooms; Irma Stern held her exhibitions there; in addition, the third-floor loft had for a long time housed hundreds of pigeons which would have to settle elsewhere.

Sandra painted a portrait of Alice Friedland, but unfortunately it was stolen from the gallery. There is no photograph of it.

This second painting, is as alive as The Blue Bathroom *with its brightly coloured washing on the line. There were always washing lines fluttering with colour in District Six backyards, and home-made pigeon lofts were very popular.*

NEWSPAPER CRITICS present at Sandra's s exhibition wrote that they were confused by Sandra's different styles: her London work in contrast to her District Six work. André Cilliers, writing in the Cape Times on August 27, 1963, was particularly aware of this.

MIXTURE OF STYLES IN ARTIST'S SHOW

… Her approach varies from that of the "society portrait" in the manner of De Laszlo and John Singer Sargent to genre subjects, done in a "poor man's Van Gogh" way…

… Too little attention is given to the grey element in all colour in Nature; too much pure colour is used. "Blue Cart" (No. 35) is a case in point. The fact that the cart is blue is overstated to an absurd degree. It would not matter so much if the artist did not prove she has considerable talent. One cannot dismiss her.

To confuse a poor critic even more, the almost austere restraint of a picture like "La Madre" (No. 49) shows how powerful this artist can be if she curbs her exuberance. The portraits "Maria Gloria" (No. 56) and "Anders Timburg" (No. 48)

The haunted stair
1963
60 x 50cm
Pen. sepia ink and gouache
Signed bottom left

Inscribed at base: *Sandra McGregor 1963 "The haunted stair" Old staircase – Regency Art Gallery, Church St. Cape Town – With love to Malinda.*

MALINDA DU RANDT

Gallery staff told me that they had frequently seen a ghost on these stairs. The spectre, a blonde lady, was said to laugh heartily and mimic Alice Friedland. There was nothing sinister about this spectre's appearance apparently and I never saw her while painting this picture, although I sensed a strange atmosphere there from time to time.

are virtuoso productions in the Sargent style; the danger of slickness is only just avoided…

Eye for Material
With attention to colour, Sandra McGregor should go far, for she has an eye for pictorial material…

The ability to see pictures in unpromising material is one of this artist's assets. When she has sorted out her present confusion, we can expect to see work of a truly exciting nature.

Neville Dubow writing in the Cape Argus on 27 August 1963, also commented on the different styles in Sandra's work.

SANDRA MCGREGOR IS AN ARTIST AT THE CROSSROADS
… The first is that of popular acclaim – reproductions, perhaps, in department store windows – and commercial success…

Were this all that Sandra had to offer one would shed no tears. However, this is not the case. For over and above the optical illusionism she does show a strong capacity for characterization, an inquiring spirit and a marked degree of technical competence.

Stonier path
And this brings us to the other path which she might choose to follow – not the primrose path of clever-clever realism but the stonier one of honest naturalism without the tricks…

… In other words she is dealing here with form and not just appealing subject matter.

Now possibly a development of this approach is not going to draw the oohs and ahs that will inevitably accrue to the paintings in the first category. But it might win respect for her as an artist who has serious things to say. The choice is hers.

SANDRA CONTINUED painting in the District, regardless of what anyone said. She painted scenes which appealed to her, people who would sit for her, action that was taking place around her.

The Seven Steps was a landmark and busy gathering place. Sandra meandered through the District, often returning to the area to shelter there at Motjie Ragmat's house during the day.

A lot went on in the 'Big House' where Boss, an African man, and his

'Onse artist'

wife lived. It was notorious for its comings and goings so was often very noisy. It was an old house with many rooms, in which stolen goods were often hidden – and criminals too. The blue door was always kept securely locked. One cold winter's night, Sandra and Motjie Ragmat watched police entering the 'Big House'. It was dark and the police lights showed up in a most dramatic way. Then they saw that the police had dogs with them and Motjie Ragmat said they were after men with drugs.

Boss knew Sandra, had often seen her going in and out of Motjie Ragmat's house, and had noticed her painting in the District. When Sandra told him she wanted to paint the interior of the 'Big House', he agreed. She stood just inside the entrance, knowing that it was an honour to be invited into this infamous house.

THE DKS (DYNAMITE KIDS) and their arch enemies the Stalag 17s were the leading gangs in District Six from the 1960s onwards. The Stalag 17s lived in a notorious old building called 'The Winter Gardens' in Ayre Street. There were often fights between these two gangs. Motjie Ragmat told Sandra of a dreadful happening between them. They had agreed to meet at a certain spot for a picnic. No weapons would be allowed. But the Stalag 17s brought weapons. The leader of the DKs was made to stand in the centre of a circle of men holding pangas and knives and he had to try and break through them. He was brutally murdered.

Sandra herself once saw the Stalag 17s ready to do battle again – all armed with pangas and knives. She was in Motjie Ragmat's house at the time, and she watched them streaming past the Seven Steps on their way to Hanover Street.

Walking in District Six one day, Sandra noticed a strange atmosphere and hostility from a group of men – 'skollies' – seated on the pavement at the corner where the DKs gathered. Not one of them said a word. Motjie Ragmat told Sandra they were dangerous. They had attacked and raped a white prison wardress near Roeland Street Prison. The wardress wore spectacles which were knocked off her face, so she could not see her attackers. In court, she told the police that the gang was coloured, but she could not identify the gang members. The DKs' main leaders had been arrested and imprisoned.

Sandra ignored Motjie Ragmat's warning and early the following morning she walked slowly up Caledon Street – wearing her usual jeans, thick leather belt and bright shirt – carrying her basket of paint brushes.

Backyard in Caledon Street
1960s
37 x 18cm
Pen, sepia ink and gouache on paper
Signed bottom right

PRIVATE COLLECTION

Children often idled in backyards or on the streets. With no toys to play with they created their own games and often made toys from what they could find.

The space under the stairs was used sometimes for storage, sometimes as a sleeping place.

Children often wanted to be included in my pictures and that's why the little girl on the stairs is waving at me.

> *I greeted them with a smile and this time they smiled back.
> I heard one say to the others, "Sy's die artist." I told the man they called Amaar he'd be wonderful to paint. Amaar was sitting on the pavement wearing a bright red shirt and he had a gold earring in one ear. He agreed to pose for a portrait. Motjie Ragmat was angry when she heard about this and said that the men were in an ugly mood.*

Sandra came to know many of the 'skollies' and often asked them to pose for her. They admired her courage and did not feel threatened by her in any way. These dangerous men became her protectors.

SANDRA RECORDED the old carts too, many of varying colours, then still used by hawkers in the District. In *Three Carts*, the juxtaposition of colours intrigued her, and Sandra included the painting in her first solo exhibition.

The other 'carts' of District Six were not carts at all, but carriages, drawn by white horses for Malay weddings, reminiscent of the *carrozelle* in Italy. Sandra visited the stables in District Six and in the Malay Quarter: those in District Six were demolished before she could paint them. Often Sandra stayed on for supper with one of the families she knew in the District.

> *The sounds linger with me now, the call of the snoek cart, the old horse coming up Hanover Street, pulling a fruit and vegetable cart...
> I can see my favourite cart which I thought was so beautiful.*

To prevent theft, the wheels were removed at night and replaced again in the morning. Sandra recalls that this painting was acquired by a local man whose parents had lived in the East End of London, and had sold iron from a cart. It is not known if they made a success of selling scrap iron, but they eventually left England and came to settle in Cape Town, bequeathing substantial sums of money to the poor.

IN THOSE FIRST MAGICAL DAYS in 1962, Buck took Sandra to Vernon Terrace. Vernon Terrace never lost its intrigue for Sandra, and she painted there often.

The 'smous', an old-clothes dealer, was a well known figure in the District; children knew his call and came running to him. With a sack over his shoulder he would knock on doors, hoping to buy or sell. Mr Hartley's tailor shop was on the right of the arch, but is not visible in the painting. He was the first person in the District to look after Sandra's art equipment

Three Carts

1962/3
38 x 51cm
Pen, sepia ink and gouache
No visible signature

OWNER UNKNOWN

Reproduced from a photographic print

These three carts were standing at the sandy, side entrance to Vernon Terrace, in front of a small house whose walls were light grey with touches of pale blue and pink. What appealed to me was the contrast between the mauve and purple shadows and the dark green carts with their red wheels.

Life at the Seven Steps – daytime
1963
110 x 50cm
Panel – oil on board
Signed bottom left

JULIAN ADLER

A series of steps led up from Hanover Street to Caledon Street, and this whole area – known as the Seven Steps – was a popular, well-used thoroughfare. Mothers met to gossip, children played at their feet, men loitered, drank or fought, residents leaned out of their windows to watch.

Boss, whom I came to know well, lived in the 'Big House' on the top floor, and spent much of his time leaning out of the window watching the street.

RIGHT

The banisters and newel post in Staircase in the 'Big House' were made of a beautiful honey-coloured wood. Boss allowed me to wander, even to go upstairs to the first floor where it was dark and I could hear rats scuffling in the corners.

FAR RIGHT

In Stairs with little girl I painted the stairs again with a little girl who had been born in the 'Big House', standing at the foot of the stairs. She told me she had heard a noise downstairs, and came to look. I asked her to stand there and pose.

'Onse artist'

Staircase in the 'Big House'
1963
110 x 50cm
Panel – oil on board
No visible signature

OWNER UNKNOWN

Reproduced from a photographic print

Stairs with little girl
1963
110 x 50cm
Panel – oil on board
No visible signature

OWNER UNKNOWN

Reproduced from a photographic print

Sandra McGregor – 'Onse artist' in District Six

Sandra McGregor – 'Onse artist' in District Six

Man with broken bottle
1960s
estimated 40 x 32cm
Pen, black ink and gouache
Signed top right

PRIVATE COLLECTION

It was seldom peaceful at the Seven Steps and fights broke out frequently, usually after much drinking The atmosphere in my picture is tense but there are groups of men unconcerned with what is happening.
It could be dangerous to interfere.

The door to Motjie Ragmat's house is on the left at the top of these steps, and also on the left at the bottom, the door near the stone parapet leads to Cass's house.

overnight. His helper, Omar, would bring it out each morning for Sandra to continue painting this scene, and collect it in the evening.

Over the years different communities had once lived in Vernon Terrace – officers from the garrison at the Castle, Jewish residents, and in Sandra's time, coloured people. Whoever lived there, the strong residential element remained. People were friendly, communities mixed, children played together and much of life was lived in the street.

One summer's afternoon in Vernon Terrace, I stood painting a large picture on my easel. As usual, I was surrounded by a crowd of excited children. Suddenly there was a deafening noise and a run-away horse and cart bore down on us. We all scattered. To my surprise, dear Mrs Manshun, who lived in one of the houses, ignoring the hooves of the bolting horse, rushed into its path and grabbed my easel and painting just in time to save them from destruction. She became a good friend of mine.

SANDRA BECAME a well known figure in the District, and young and old enjoyed being part of her work. She in turn showed great interest in and understanding of their lives. In a letter to the press written in 1966, entitled 'Painter finds great heart in District Six', Sandra, in the paragraph quoted below, shows her sensitivity and appreciation of a 'way of life' she came to love.

District Six has a language of its own, and beneath the joy and the sorrow, the laughter and the tears, a mighty heart is beating.
It is not an area – it is a way of life. A way of life in which the artist is privileged to share.

The children of District Six, in particular, knew Sandra well and loved to be with her. These were the children of poor parents, rushing to welcome her every morning, gathering about her, chanting, *"Hier kom Sandera! Hier kom Sandera! Kyk haar kwassies en die stoel. Paint my af, Miss Sandera, paint my af."* They delighted in helping carry the heavy art equipment to wherever she was going to paint. They clustered round as close as they could, watching as she worked and eyeing the gouache colours on her palette. Often Sandra used an umbrella to shade her palette to stop the paints drying too fast. But even so, when she was finished, she still had to scrape off the dried-up remnants with a palette knife.

Then the children would pounce to get a flake of colour, hold it under

'Onse artist'

the tap and then paint on bits of old newspaper. In Combrink and Russell Streets the children painted on the pavements which gave them a good flat surface.

I remember the children from the early sixties: Arthur, Ronnie, Toyer, Henry, Alfie, Armien, and so many others. I was so grateful to them for their help. Painting 'on the spot' was a wonderful experience, but without the children of District Six, I could not have managed. Just as I could not have managed without my dear Motjie Rachmat and her wonderful kindness.

BRUCE HEILBUTH, writing in the press in August 1966, called Sandra:
PIED PIPER OF ART IN DISTRICT 6
She has spent almost every day for three years wandering there, stopping to paint or draw when a face or feature catches her eye.

Her small figure, her jeans and ponytail are recognised everywhere. Windows open, street-corner loungers nod and smile and the children come running whenever she passes. 'Good morning, artist,' they say, 'will you paint me today?'

"I think District 6 is the most honest place I have known. Because so many of the people have nothing, they have nothing to hide. There is no hypocrisy. And yet they have taught me that the poor can have tremendous spiritual wealth…"

Living alone, without family or children of her own, Sandra loved these children and their joyous attitude to life. She sometimes watched them at play, making do with whatever they could find. She found it uplifting and inspiring.

I often watched the children of the Seven Steps having the most wonderful joy and happiness playing with their simple toys. In District Six a favourite game was to have an empty cardboard box. One small child would get into the box at the top of the steps and the other children would give the box a mighty push – they would scream with joy as the box went thumpedy-thumpedy-thump to the bottom step. With much laughter the box would be carried to the top step, and another child would get into it and the whole process would be repeated, with much shouting and enjoyment.

Sometimes I would see the children playing games with pieces of string that they had found on the field or in the gutter, and stones of

---

The Seven Steps - woman with curlers
1960s
39 x 29cm
Gouache on paper
Signed 'Sandra' bottom left

CINDY YEOMAN

*I drew this soon after the man with the bottle had gone.
A woman with curlers in her hair came out to see what the noise was all about, but life carried on as if nothing had happened*

Sandra's favourite cart
1963
110 x 50cm
Panel – oil on board
No visible signature

OWNER UNKNOWN

This painting was reproduced on the poster for my first exhibition at the Regency Gallery, Cape Town in 1963. I loved the small painted flowers on the side of the cart and the bright cadmium red of the harnessing poles with their blue tips. The cart was propped against a wall in Clifton Street – a marvellous yellow-orange wall. Real van Gogh! Cart-owners would remove the wheels at night and put them back the next day.

  I liked the diagonal format of the cart in this composition because it's so dynamic even without wheels. And the colour was irresistible – brightly coloured washing hanging on the line – a trademark of District Six – and the gaily-painted cart help balance the image.

An old cart
1963
110 x 50cm
Panel – oil on board
No visible signature

PRIVATE COLLECTION

Reproduced from a photographic print

Some carts were not beautiful. This old cart, with its wheels attached, was possibly abandoned and had seen better days when I found it.

Sandra McGregor – 'Onse artist' in District Six

Vernon Terrace
1963
40 x 50cm
Sepia ink and gouache
Signed top left

MANUELA ZUIDEMA

Through the archway, on the left is the blue-green front door of Mrs Scholz, and stairs lead up to a small square of colourful terrace houses. Mrs Manshun lived in one of these. Red Roses Hairdressing & Shaving Saloon was a well-patronised establishment in the District.

Pieter Breughel's paintings have always fascinated me and and I loved depicting similar scenes: busy with people and life and a story to tell. Here I used pen and sepia ink with yellow ochre and raw sienna gouache.

different shapes. One morning they were gathered together and I went to see what was causing them such interest – only to find a dead rat that they were prodding with a long stick!

Another afternoon I remember clearly. It had been raining hard and one could see the streams of water running down the mountain. I noticed a small crowd of children gathered together, and as I got nearer I saw they were gathered round a little boy who was kneeling in the gutter, drinking the flowing water. When he saw me he said, with such excitement, "Dis water van die Berg, Miss artist, dis water van die Berg!"

◆

Sandra McGregor – 'Onse artist' in District Six

CHAPTER 10

The best of times

Sandra painting in District Six.

In 1964 Sandra was commissioned by the general manager of the Grand Hotel, Anatole Urbaniak, to paint twenty-five panels for the hotel which stood on the corner of Adderley and Strand Streets in the centre of Cape Town. This prestigious eleven-storey building was first opened at the end of 1893 by the Castle Line. The original hotel had a 250 foot frontage, which was the longest of any hotel in South Africa. Anatole Urbaniak, a former Polish military man with typical officer bearing, ran the hotel like clockwork. Sandra had been at Roedean School with Urbaniak's wife, Jennifer (née Denoon-Duncan), and was delighted to have the challenge.

The panels, 100 x 50cm, were painted in oil on board and represented a series of uniquely personal glimpses of life in District Six. The subjects – interiors and exteriors – ranged from backyards, kitchens, staircases, washing poles and lines, street scenes, to portraits. These paintings were displayed in the Grand Hotel until the hotel was demolished in 1972, to make way for a Woolworths building.

As I would settle down to draw the children clustered like bees round a honeypot. I never chased them away, asking only that they should not obstruct my view.

They were the most delightful children I have ever met, anywhere … so utterly unspoiled and natural … What a joy it was for an artist to find so many people in one place, who simply loved to pose.

Urbaniak had bought the twenty-five panels for R250. Before demolition, Julian Adler at Sandra's request asked Urbaniak to sell back all the panels. A price of R600 was agreed. Over the years these paintings have been sold, dispersed far and wide. In the last decade fourteen of the originals have been located and photographs found of the remaining eleven.

In 2006 four old Roedeanians bought three panels from Sandra to give to Roedean School, and another was purchased by the SAORA (SA Old Roedeanian Association): *Die Hokke at the Seven Steps*; *Portrait of Gadija, an Indian girl*; *Backyard behind Hadji's house* and *Portrait of Cass in Hadj robes*.

ANOTHER PANEL, a particular favourite of Sandra's, *The Blue Door,* is of a small backyard in District Six. It has the usual wooden step at the entrance and the door leading into the yard is painted a dramatic blue.

> *Whilst I stood looking at the colourful composition, an old lady appeared and she was so excited that I had chosen to paint her yard. I knew that this picture would take a full week to paint, if not more. But my new friend assured me that the yard would be left exactly as it was, nothing would be touched. This was another example of the kindness of my District Six friends and the lengths to which they would go to assist me.*

The Blue Door
1964/65
110 x 50cm
Panel – oil on board
No visible signature

OWNER UNKNOWN

Reproduced from a photographic print

At the back of the yard was a cupboard painted the same blue as the door and stacked with old bottles, tins and boxes. I was attracted by its bright colours. It had the usual table, basins and a solitary tap

The best of times

Die Hokke *at the Seven Steps*
1964/65
110 x 50cm
Panel – oil on board
No visible signature

ROEDEAN SCHOOL (SA)

Reproduced from a photographic print

Die Hokke was a secluded wooden shed where stolen goods were often stored. This shed stood in a small unfrequented alleyway, between the 'Big House' at the Seven Steps and the house in which Cass lived with his parents, Mareldia and Ishmail. All sorts of people went in and out of this shed on their often nefarious business.

Portrait of Gadija, an Indian girl
1964/65
110 x 50cm
Panel – oil on board
Signed top left

ROEDEAN SCHOOL (SA)

Gadija, a friend of Cass's, was one of the few Indians who lived in the District. I enjoyed painting her because she was such a willing sitter. Always gracious and distinctive in colourful saris, she honoured the customs of her culture.

The best of times

Backyard behind Hadji's house
1964/65
110 x 50cm
Panel – oil on board
Signed bottom right

ROEDEAN SCHOOL (SA)

Reproduced from a photographic print

This was painted in Hadji's backyard, near that of Motjie Ragmat. At the top of the stairs was a room where Doos's aunt lived. Doos was an escaped prisoner who hid there and appears in several of my paintings, often wearing grey trousers, a blue and white sweater and a grey hat.

IN DECEMBER 1967 the Dean of Cape Town, the Very Reverend EL (Ted) King consented to Sandra holding an exhibition of her paintings in St George's Cathedral. This was her second exhibition. Most of the work was of District Six and included the commissioned panels, before installation in the Grand Hotel.

I thought it would be a wonderful idea to take some of the subjects of my paintings to view this exhibition. None of them had ever been in the Cathedral – they were all Muslims. They refused to go by bus, so I walked with them from Hanover Street. My friends were overwhelmed by the beauty of the Cathedral. It was a lovely summer's day and I enjoyed explaining to them the symbolism in the stained glass windows by the renowned Gabriel Loire.

In the Cape Argus on 18 December 1967 George Manuel wrote:

'HEY, MAN, LOOK AT US IN THE CATHEDRAL'

It was a red letter day in the lives of eight District Six boys. They had been invited by the artist Sandra McGregor to view her exhibition of paintings in St. George's Cathedral.

At first they were hesitant. One said he doubted whether Coloured people would be allowed within the precincts of so important a place of worship.

Another said they were too poorly dressed and would be turned away.

Miss McGregor assured them that their fears were unfounded. She told them that she wanted them to see the paintings for which they had posed.

… Led by Manna, the tallest, they entered the Cathedral door shyly. They were ill at ease when they found themselves inside the cool, quiet, high-roofed building. It was obvious they would have been more at home in a cinema in District Six, attending a matinée.

Then they spotted one of the paintings of a cinema, outside which they usually congregate. There, in rich hues, they were all depicted. Excitedly they pointed one another out.

There was old Mantjie, old Eitjie and Baillie. Manne, Amaar and Bones. All in a painting!

It was eight happy corner boys who hurried back to District Six later that day to tell with pride that their pictures were hanging on the sacred walls.

… No one could have shown these rough diamonds of District

Six a better Christmas gesture of goodwill than Miss McGregor on that day.

In an article in the Cape Argus, 20 December 1967, a large accompanying picture shows Sandra with two of her friends, Maantjie and Manne, viewing her paintings in the Cathedral. They are smiling at the sight of paintings done by 'Onse artist, Miss Sandera'. Sandra is wearing her precious 'skollie' belt with 121 studs, which can be clearly seen. Her 'skollie' friends in Caledon Street had made it for her. She bought the black leather belt and they hammered in the studs. These belts made dangerous weapons and ultimately the 'skollies' were forbidden wearing them by the police. Sandra used to walk past the police station in Caledon Street, proud of being the only person in Cape Town who was allowed to wear such a belt! She still treasures it. George Manuel caught the spirit of that occasion:

CROWD SCENES

… Visit the Cathedral and see her (Sandra's) District Six scenes in rich colours and much detail.

… District Six is a part of Cape Town that is noted for its crowd scenes. You see crowds in and outside barber shops, congregated outside the cinemas, on the pavements and on the stoeps.

Sandra has captured this atmosphere of 'crowdedness'. If you, seeing her pictures, are inclined to regard them as having too many figures in them remember that Sandra has painted what she saw and those who know the place well will give you full marks.

THE EXHIBITION drew a strange letter to the press, published on 11 January 1968, and written by a visitor to the Cape.

Visitors are critical

ART AND JEANS AT ST. GEORGE'S

To the Editor, The Argus

Sir, – We have visited your lovely country twice before and now our third visit has perhaps been the most enjoyable of them all. But we are surprised at many things we have heard and seen during the time we have been here.

We were surprised to see the non-Europeans so often attending church services and seemingly so happy.

We were surprised to hear most of them speaking English. We

Ayre Street	*Die Kraal,* Ayre Street	*Hadji's backyard in bright sunshine*
1964/65	1964/65	1964/65
110 x 50cm	110 x 50cm	110 x 50cm
Panel – oil on board	Panel – oil on board	Panel – oil on board
Signed bottom left	No visible signature	No visible signature
JULIAN ADLER	OWNER UNKNOWN	OWNER UNKNOWN

This is a typical domestic washday scene. Women usually washed clothes in basins in their backyards, but here they are using an open-air trough

There was always thick mud in front of this house, possibly due to the overflow from a nearby washing trough.

There was a nook under the stairway in Hadji's backyard where (another) Gadija, 'the ugliest woman in District Six' slept. Gadija had won this remarkable title in a competition!

The best of times

Atta's kitchen

1964/65
110 x 50cm
Panel – oil on board
Signed bottom right

ANGLICAN CHURCH
OF SOUTHERN AFRICA

Atta, an elderly washerwoman, was Motjie Ragmat's cousin. She always had a pot of coffee on her primus stove. One day I knocked on Atta's door: I was carrying my easel and a big basket of painting equipment. The children opened the door and said, "No thank you, no old clothes!" I painted the interior of the kitchen, and included the three children playing a game.

Backyard with basins

1964/65
110 x 50cm
Panel – oil on board
Signed bottom right

ANGLICAN CHURCH
OF SOUTHERN AFRICA

This was a typical small backyard, usually with one tap, a table and basins. The long pole (branch of a tree) was used for stringing the washing line up high, so that the washing could dry and not become soiled.

List of twenty-five panels first exhibited at St George's Cathedral, Cape Town, in 1965, before being hung in the Grand Hotel in Strand Street:

1	Buck's Chair	61
2	Malay Quarter rooftops in sunlight	63
3	Malay Quarter rooftops as the sun is setting	63
4	The Black Trunk	65
5	Sandra's Kloof Street studio	66
6	Motjie Ragmat's kitchen	76
7	Motjie Ragmat's backyard leading to Caledon Street	77
8	Portrait of Rashied, Motjie Ragmat's grandson	78
9	Portrait of Cass in Hadj robes	79
10	Portrait of Cass with red lantern	79
11	Portrait of Cass	80
12	Life at the Seven Steps – daytime	94
13	Staircase in the 'Big House'	95
14	Stairs with little girl	95
15	Sandra's favourite cart	100
16	An old cart	101
17	The Blue Door	106
18	Die Hokke at the Seven Steps	107
19	Portrait of Gadija, an Indian girl	108
20	Backyard behind Hadji's house	109
21	Ayre Street	112
22	Die Kraal, Ayre Street	112
23	Hadji's backyard in bright sunshine	112
24	Atta's Kitchen	113
25	Backyard with basins	113

had thought Afrikaans was their language.

As regular churchgoers we were astonished to see a group of pictures for sale in your lovely Anglican Cathedral.

Surely there are studios in town to be rented for artists to display their pictures for sale.

Christ did not tolerate money-changers in the temple.

At the same cathedral we were astonished to see a young woman wearing tight jeans at the Eucharist. We have never seen this, even in the U.S.A.

God's house and the church's sacraments should not be so disregarded.

We were told by some of the congregation that they did not like to see this form of dress at the Eucharist.

M and J.E. HETHERINGTON – Sea Point

The Dean of Cape Town responded as follows:
> The recent exhibition of pictures in the cathedral was held to stress the fact that all man's artistic striving is essentially God-centred and that the church is not confined to what is sometimes called religious art.
>
> The pictures here were, in fact, painted by a member of the cathedral congregation and the fact that two or three of them were, I believe, subsequently sold, merely highlights the fact that they were duly appreciated. They weren't auctioned in the cathedral, if this is the implication.
>
> The fact that a young woman in the cathedral habitually worships in tight jeans is to me, and I hope to most other Christians, a matter of momentous indifference.
>
> God wants us as we are and, as far as I know, the young lady in question always wears jeans and was, in fact, confirmed by the Bishop in jeans not so very long ago.
>
> Where the church has so often failed is in being precisely a conclave of the respectable and not a family as various as the human race.

ONE DAY, walking down Caledon Street, Sandra passed a small hairdressing shop. In the corner sat a man busily working at a tapestry. He gave her a broad smile – he knew her from her basket full of paintbrushes – and

Portrait of Charlie
1964/65
76 x 51cm
Cray-pas on strawboard
Signed top right

PRIVATE COLLECTION

Charlie chose to wear an exotic eastern gown of deep blue silk, with dragons embroidered down the front in silver and gold. He also wore dramatic long earrings and posed well.

The best of times

Portrait of Hadji
1964/65
73 x 49cm
Cray-pas on strawboard
Signed bottom left

JULIAN ADLER

Everyone knew the sitter as Hadji. He was the husband of a woman who lived next door to Motjie Ragmat. A quiet and peaceful man, he had made the journey to Mecca and sat for me wearing his Hadj clothes. I never did know his real name.

The best of times

Portrait of Kaye
1964/65
73 x 49cm
Cray-pas on strawboard
No visible signature

PRIVATE COLLECTION

Round the walls of his room were all kinds of clothes – mainly long evening dresses. He wanted to be painted wearing one of these, and asked if he should wear make-up. It was very hot and he was shirtless and I said no, I wanted to paint him as he was. He wore eye make-up only and round his neck a blue amulet that someone had given him. His hands were powerful and spoke of strange things and he wanted them crossed over his chest.

117

Sandra McGregor – 'Onse artist' in District Six

Portrait of Duke with hammer
1965
75 x 50cm
Cray-pas on strawboard
Signed bottom right

PRIVATE COLLECTION

Duke was dark-skinned, with good features, a beard and dark piercing eyes. I decided to use cray-pas on strawboard to suit his colouring. In the first of two portraits I painted, he wore a heavy green sweater, and his dark skin contrasted well with this. As he was a carpenter, I suggested he hold a hammer in his hand.

RIGHT
In the second sitting I asked him to hold a large flagon of wine. He agreed, but only if the wine consisted of red crystals and water – the sweet red drink that mothers made for children in District Six. I only learnt later that he was a heavy drinker. In this portrait his shirt, open at the throat, revealed a gold medallion which he always wore.

Portrait of Duke with flagon
1965
75 x 50cm
Cray-pas on strawboard
Signed bottom right
Inscription on label on reverse: 'Duke of Hanover St. 1965'

PRIVATE COLLECTION

introduced himself as Charlie. The other man in the shop was cutting a client's hair, and he said, "Hello, I'm Kaye."

Sandra asked Charlie if he would pose for a portrait. He agreed and they worked in Cass's house at the Seven Steps. It was summertime so they had the window open – and the children of the Seven Steps enjoyed watching Sandra paint Charlie's portrait, teasing him and calling him – "Jou moffie!" He was gay, and everyone knew it. This tolerance was something else Sandra learnt about District Six: that everyone was accepted as they were. There was no need to hide behind masks and veils. White South African society at the time was far less tolerant and less accepting of homosexuality.

During Sandra's early years in District Six she had few clothes and could not afford to buy new shirts which she badly needed. One day as she passed Charlie's shop, he handed her a brown paper parcel. She opened it excitedly and to her surprise it contained two brightly coloured shirts.

Charlie had realised my need, and had acted accordingly. He said it was because I always seemed to wear the same ones. I treasured those shirts and wore them for many years.

Kaye, equally charming, worked for Charlie. Sandra painted his portrait in the backyard room of a little house in Woodstock where he lived.

In 1980 the last of the buildings I drew and painted, came down. My friends, then, were scattered far and wide. But occasionally I would see Charlie sitting in St. George's Cathedral. One day, on a Groote Schuur bus, who should I see but Kaye, looking very smart in a suit, collar and tie!

ONE COLD WINTER'S DAY as Sandra sat painting at the Seven Steps, she became aware of an enormous rough-looking man watching with great interest what she was doing. As she was packing away her paints and brushes, she asked him about himself. His name was Duke and he spoke excellent English, with an American accent, and had spent some years in the merchant navy. Sandra said he would make a fine model. He agreed to sit for a portrait and came every day to Cass's house at the Seven Steps.

Sandra wanted to paint a third portrait of Duke and they were to meet at Cass's house again. It was not to be. She found him sprawled across the table dead drunk. He became ill and died not long after this.

Sandra McGregor – 'Onse artist' in District Six

CHAPTER 11

Saturday bioscope

The British Cinema
1966
Approx. 45 x 35cm
Pen, sepia ink and gouache
Signed bottom right

OWNER UNKNOWN

Mr Faber, the owner of the British, is in the box office in the second archway and is wearing a white shirt, tie, and braces. Some of the DKs are gathered outside on the corner. Amaar is in front, near the barrow, in jeans, a blue and white striped shirt and a red jersey. Manne is standing next to Mr Faber, in a white and blue shirt and a dark blue cardigan. Manne was well built, with fair skin and blue eyes. Jinx is in front in a navy and white striped shirt.

Besides portraits, Sandra painted many buildings and street scenes, and of course the cinemas. Sandra painted the four cinemas in the District. The Star Bioscope in Hanover Street; the Avalon Cinema near the top of Hanover Street; the British Cinema in Caledon Street and the National Cinema in William Street. Each cinema showed a particular type of film which attracted different kinds of people. There was no television in South Africa until 1976 and cinemas were always crowded. Saturday was bioscope day.

Sandra used pen and sepia ink and gouache for her painting of the Star – which eventually burned down. The original work has not been traced, and there is no photographic record. This building and the Avalon did not excite her as much as the other two cinemas. Despite Sandra's lack of enthusiasm for the Star Bioscope, the route to fame then in District Six was to sing on its stage in the style of crooners – Perry Como, Bing Crosby or Dean Martin. The aspiring singer had to sing in front of the most critical audience, move and reproduce the crooner's every nuance and tone. If he was no good he would be pelted with anything at hand, and booed off the stage. If he was really good, he would be applauded and then called by the name of the singer.

The Avalon was a stark building, maroon and grey, built after the war. It was called a luxury cinema because it had padded seats. The entrance doors were at street level and there were always a few boys lounging on the street corners. Although the walls were adorned with posters of films, trailer stills and photographs of actors and actresses, it was a clinical building, lacking the colour and atmosphere of the British or the National.

The British Cinema was a distinctive green building with three imposing arches. This cinema showed mainly cowboy films and thrillers – films the gangs loved. It took Sandra almost three weeks to paint the British Cinema and involved much drawing, particularly the perspective of the pole and telephone lines. The painting was sold for R10 when Sandra needed money.

One gang member, Jinx, was painted several times by Sandra. He was knifed to death some months after Sandra finished the painting. He had betrayed the DKs to another gang – an unforgiveable offence. One of the DKs had followed Jinx one night and stabbed a knife through his heart.

Many people knew Claude, a young man who pushed his barrow of fruit – apples, pears, bananas, whatever was in season – and parked it in various places. It is visible in Sandra's painting of the British Cinema, and Sandra often saw it parked in Caledon Street, and on cold nights outside Millers Fish & Chip Shop.

The corner view of the British Cinema is also full of bustling Saturday afternoon life. Sandra's method of painting these scenes, in pen and ink and gouache, was meticulous.

> *First the entire composition for the British Cinema was drawn in great detail in pencil. This was then fixed with fixative. Then I drew over it all again with sepia ink and a very fine nib. I also drew in sepia ink the 'lines of direction', showing perspective and texture. For example, the texture of the buildings, the shadows, the pole (it has to look round and solid at the drawing stage). Only then did I begin to colour, starting at the back and working forwards, so that the colours at the front were applied last. The figures who posed for me stood still while I drew them.*
>
> *All the hard work is in the drawing. Shadows are painted in very lightly. They have to look pale and transparent. Their shape has already been drawn in. Note that the pole is off-centre. Never have anything right in the centre.*

SANDRA'S FAVOURITE was the National Cinema and she painted it several times. Built in 1908 in William Street, the National was a fine example of Edwardian architecture. The architecture was more complex than that of the British Cinema. The oldest opera house in Cape Town, it was known as the National Theatre for many years, but originally it had been called the Gaiety Theatre. District Six in the early 1900s was still a predominantly white residential area. It had an orchestra pit, stalls, upper circle, and even the 'gods'. Upstairs were dressing rooms with red velvet on the walls for artists, actors and singers.

The National Cinema still had an old-fashioned air of elegance when Sandra first painted it in 1967. In common with the British Cinema painting, there is much activity: people are standing in groups, talking, and there are children in the street.

The wall of the building in this painting is particularly significant as it reveals a technique which Sandra often used.

> *I applied the colour and obtained the speckled effect by dipping a toothbrush into paint which I had put into a saucer. Then I ran my finger along the bristles to spray paint on to the image. This particular painting sold for R20.*

The National was a meeting place where Broertjie and his gang often

The British Cinema sideways on
circa 1966
43 x 33cm
Pen, sepia ink and gouache
Signed bottom right

DIANE FAIRHEAD

Mr Faber is here again, hands in pockets, wearing the same clothes and standing near the box office. The DKs, with their studded 'skollie' belts would always be lounging about, often with clinging girls in tow.

There was never a shortage of characters to fill my pictures, and Table Mountain with the old cableway station provided an ideal background.

Saturday bioscope

gathered. They would appear around eleven in the morning. In this painting, Broertjie is wearing a white shirt, and Aisa, whom he later married, is with him. Broertjie worked at the docks in ships' holds, handling frozen fish. Sandra subsequently visited him in Pollsmoor. In later life he developed serious asthma and his wife had to work to support both of them. The man with the red striped shirt on the right is Arthur, who loved to sing. Sandra had met Arthur by chance, practising for the Carnival.

> At 'Coon Carnival' time, when the various troupes were practising, walking home one night in the dark, through the windows I saw the glow of lamps and candles. As I approached a house I noticed the door was slightly open, and I heard singing. I knocked and went inside.
> In the dark room lit only by a lamp, I saw a circle of my 'skollie' friends. They were practicing for the 'Coon Carnival'. There was only one chair which they insisted I take. They were all seated on the floor or standing.
>
> Arthur, one of the 'Coons' who was standing, said, "Miss artist, I shall sing a song for you." At that time The Sound of Music was showing in Cape Town, and with no musical accompaniment he sang one of the songs, Climb Every Mountain. Besides a fine voice he sang with such feeling that I shall never forget it. At the end of the song he said, "Miss Sandra, that is a gift to you from the heart of a 'skollie' in District Six."

THE 'COON CARNIVAL' was the major event of the year. Thousands of men, known colloquially as the 'Coons', marched from the top of Hanover Street to Green Point Stadium to take part in a huge annual singing and dancing competition. Months of rehearsals and preparation, in backyards and dingy rooms, preceded this challenge. Many of Sandra's friends were members of various troupes. They wore magnificent costumes, in bright shiny colours, and there was great rivalry between the troupes for the prized silver cups.

> All the way up Hanover Street small flags were draped on high from lamp post to lamp post, adding more colour to the excited atmosphere. The pavements were crowded, the children tried to wriggle their way, pushing and pulling, through the adults, who were fighting to keep their places in the seething mass. It was mid-summer and extremely warm, and the hot sun caused much friction. At last, to shouts and applause, the 'Coons' appeared – completely filling Hanover Street.
>
> The music, the song, the dance, the excitement, the laughter, the tears made it one of the most exciting events that I have ever seen. Only the great carnivals in Italy, in Florence, Sienna and in Rio, could be

Saturday bioscope

The National Cinema
1967
34 x 45cm
Pen, sepia ink and gouache on paper
No visible signature

HEATHER EDWARDS

Members of Broertjie's gang used to gather here. The girl in the blue uniform with the red tie was in the Church Brigade of Father John da Costa, priest at St Mark's Church, District Six. An Indian woman is walking down William Street towards town. Life is unhurried.

> *compared, but here the pulse-beat of Africa adds a difference, not suave and sophisticated, but fierce and almost primeval. No-one watching the 'Coon Carnival' could fail to be deeply moved.*

IN 1965 SANDRA LEFT Kloof Street and moved into a flat in Military Road, Tamboerskloof. The flat had good light, with a bedroom, bathroom and a kitchen which opened into a courtyard. It was here that she painted an early self-portrait in oil, largely encouraged by Buck. But it was not long before she moved again, this time to a flat on the top floor of Chapmill Court in St Quinton's Road, Gardens, opposite the de Waal Hotel. This flat was full of sunshine and had a fine view of the docks. She loved living there, and stayed for sixteen years until the whole block was sold in 1982. Her final move was to Morlea Court, in Rugley Road, Vredehoek.

In another self-portrait Sandra included a small carved African wooden figure behind her. This portrait was bought on behalf of Gregoire Boonzaier by Alex Rose-Innes for R25. There is no record of this painting and its whereabouts is unknown.

SOON AFTER SANDRA had settled in Chapmill Court, Father Fred Marks, the priest at St Cyprian's Anglican Church, a modest thatched building in Station Road, Retreat, asked Sandra to make a cross for his church. The brief was wide open: she could design it as she wished. Sandra consulted *St Francis of Assisi, a Pictorial Biography* by Leonard von Matt and Walter Hauser, (Longmans Green & Co. 1956.) and she based her work on the Cross of St Francis, painted by a Syrian monk at the end of the 12th century.

The purpose of the original cross – approximately 6 feet tall by four feet wide (190 x 120cm) – was to teach the meaning of the story of the crucifixion, resurrection, and ascension of Christ, and thereby strengthen the faith of the people. Throughout the centuries, this Franciscan cross has symbolized a mission to bring renewal to the Church. In Holy Week of 1957 this ancient cross was placed on public view for the first time over the new Altar in San Georgio's Chapel in the Basilica of St Clare of Assisi.

For Sandra, this was a wonderful commission and she followed the St Francis Cross closely. The illustration was in black and white, so Sandra was able to choose all the colours herself: a challenge, but what a wonderful one. John da Costa from St Mark's Church, a friend of Fred Marks, had the heavy wooden cross cut and assembled in District Six, and he heaved the cross on his shoulder up three flights of stairs to Sandra's studio in Chapmill Court.

First I primed the cross with white primer to prevent over-painting from being absorbed into the wood. Next, I drew accurate outlines in pencil, which were then fixed. I then painted over these lines using blue tempera paint, in order to create a half-tone for every outline when I applied further colour. Then I started painting. I used only Winsor and Newton artists' oil colours.

I could not afford expensive gold paint or gold leaf to create the halos, so I bought sheets of self-adhesive gold embossed paper from Sam Newman's hardware and art shop in Burg Street. I cut the required small shapes and removed the backing, and placed each sticky piece into its allotted place. For me it was an intricate labour of love.

SANDRA'S MAIN FIGURE of Jesus Christ has its own symbolism: the face is serene; the mouth is gentle; large eyes look with care and tenderness on the world. Other figures, represented in the original cross, depict characters

Sandra painting the Cross in her flat at Chapmill Court, 1966/7.

Sandra McGregor – 'Onse artist' in District Six

DETAILS OF THE CROSS

The Crucifixion: The square panel below the arms of the cross shows those present at the crucifixion of Jesus: The Virgin Mary, St John, Mary Magdelene and the other Mary and at the far right the Roman Centurion of Capernaum. The little boy on the Centurion's shoulder is his son who has been healed by Jesus. Two minor figures stand at the bottom corners of the crucifixion panel – the Roman soldier who pierced Jesus's side with a lance, and the bystander who offered Jesus a sponge soaked in common wine.

In Sandra's cross the small figure on the right is Father Liam Manning, Precentor at the Cape Town Cathedral. The figure of St John is Father Marks with his blue eyes and fair hair. The inscription above Christ's head reads
IHS NAZARE REX IUDEORU: JESUS OF NAZARETH, THE KING OF THE JEWS

The Resurrection: The central figure is of Christ risen from the dead, clad in a formal loin cloth symbolic of both high priest and victim. He stands upright, no longer hanging from nails; His eyes are open again; His face radiates an expression of peace in the knowledge that the price of our redemption is paid. He is a figure of light dominating the scene and giving light to the other figures. Behind His outstretched arms a black rectangle represents the empty tomb. The red stripe over the tomb signifies that God's love is victorious over the blackness of death. Beneath each of Christ's wrists are two angels in animated discussion and at each end of the crosspiece is a figure representing an unknown saint.

The Ascension: The rectangular panel at the top of the cross represents heaven. Emerging from a circle of red and entering heaven is Jesus, robed in garments of gold. In His left hand He carries a golden cross which is His royal sceptre and a sign of victory over death. Choirs of angels welcome Jesus into heaven. Within the red semi-circle at the top of the scene is the right hand of the Father with two fingers extended in benediction, blessing all that Jesus had done. The hand also symbolises God maintaining Creation and sending his Holy Spirit, a gift merited by Christ's sacrifice.

from the Gospel. Sandra based her figures on real people she knew. She even put in a small image of Father Liam Manning, Precentor at St George's Cathedral.

When the Cross was finished Sandra's close friends, Julian and Joyce Adler, helped her carry it downstairs and transported it in a Combi to St Cyprian's Church. The Cross was installed over the high altar and much admired.

In April 2006 I arranged a visit for Sandra and myself to the new and bigger St Cyprian's Church built just across the railway line in Retreat. The cross now hangs above the baptismal font. Father Langenhoven, the resident priest, welcomed us warmly and proudly showed us his church and the cross.

Its colours are as bright as they were when I painted it some forty years ago, due to the excellence of the paints and the fact that it had never been exposed to sunlight. I had not seen it since the day it was given over to Father Marks.

WHILE SANDRA found friendship and inspiration working in District Six, she still struggled in her private life: poverty, bulimia, and Agnes were the demons she was to battle for many years.

Poverty was always with her. She had no idea how to sell her work effectively or profitably, no idea of the cost of things, nor how to budget. She lived from day to day. She no longer had her parents' assurance that she would always be taken care of financially. Her mother helped her a little when she could, but her father did not. She was living in Chapmill Court and needed money desperately. Occasionally she sold a painting of District Six, but often sold in desperation, for as little as R10, paintings that had taken weeks of work.

She had brought back expensive clothes from England in three big trunks. She was convinced she would never wear these clothes again, especially the dresses, since she had no social life. When she did go out she wore her usual jeans, shirt, and black 'skollie' belt – something she would never sell.

One afternoon four women friends from District Six came to her flat. They were anxious to buy her clothes. Sandra had no experience whatsoever of pricing second-hand clothing. None of the dresses had been worn more than three times. One by one these beautiful dresses were sold – for R10, R8, R6 or less – and the women bought everything. All the clothes had been made by Elda Ribbetti's Florentine dressmaker: skirts, winter costumes, morning and afternoon dresses, evening dresses and an exquisite ball gown. One black dress was worn that very afternoon by one of the buyers going to a wedding.

> *The knowledge that I would never wear them again hurt, but I was so hard up I had to sell.*
>
> *I decided to sell my jewellery as well. Peter Visser bought my two pairs of Jensen earrings. I had chosen them in Copenhagen with my father, and the workmanship was exquisite. Two beautiful handbags, one black leather, lined with grey leather, the other black lined with green leather, which I bought in Amsterdam, went for very little.*

The last things she sold were her ermine stole and the black Persian lamb full-length coat which had originally belonged to her mother: Sandra happened to meet the wife of the British Consul who, as soon as she saw the furs, bought both.

The amount of money from the sale of these beautiful things was pitiful. From then on, with penury hanging over her head, Sandra was in desperate need of money. For the first time in her life she knew real poverty.

In District Six she entered the world of the poor. All her friends were poor – but they lived so generously, sharing what they had with her. There was no shame in being poor in District Six. *Kanala* – a Malay word meaning 'helping one another' – was their way of life. From the children to the old folk of District Six there flowed life, so vibrant, so exciting, that Sandra often wondered at the source of their joy. But for her, poverty was no joy at all: it continually dragged at her and still does.

Her bulimia was a different matter. For this she sought help, and although her addiction continued for many years, Sandra fought it constantly. Her attitude towards Agnes however, only deteriorated. Agnes continued to dominate her father's life. Sandra's hatred of Agnes intensified. Sandra saw her father less frequently. He had wanted his daughter to become a great portrait painter of the rich and famous, not painting portraits of coloured people – such as Charlie, Kaye, and Duke – in the poorest district in Cape Town.

CHAPTER 12

Battling the demons

At the open meetings of Alcholics Anonymous (AA), Sandra met 'Doc' de Villiers, a psychologist who had devoted his life to helping alcoholics. She also met Dudley Green, who was to have a great influence on her life. He was head of the South African Council for Alcoholism and Drug Dependence (SANCA), and a counsellor to Sandra for many years. Both men became her friends.

True to character, Sandra's father objected to her going to AA meetings, saying it was a most unsuitable place for her. He did not ask Sandra why she wanted to attend such meetings. Presumably he did not want to know.

AA taught Sandra how to deal with craving: using telephone therapy to talk and release the power of the urge; listening to the stories of other alcoholics; reading the extensive literature on the meaning of compulsion and the horror of addiction; resisting the urge a day at a time.

As part of the AA experience, Sandra was asked to accompany a former alcoholic who was visiting a man on a bender. The man's flat was an indescribable mess with empty bottles scattered everywhere, and the man himself was in a dreadful state. Sandra was horrified at the effects of addiction and watched the way her companion dealt with this man.

Sandra also firmly believed in the power of God to help an addict through prayer. In this way she began her long and arduous search for a cure.

BUCK'S SUPPORT during Sandra's early years in Cape Town was vital, but when he was transferred to Durban Sandra felt isolated once again. She had never developed a sense of responsibility for herself, always turning to someone to help her. After Buck left she realised that she needed other help.

Besides struggling with her bulimia, Sandra's relationship with Agnes deteriorated over the years. Small incidents became inflated and caused hateful reactions in Sandra: a precious book returned to her father mysteriously disappeared from the shelf where Sandra had put it, and she accused Agnes of taking it; an unreasonable request from her father to give her own opal earrings, bought in Bond Street, to Agnes, as she had endured a deprived childhood; murderous looks from Agnes when her father sat next to Sandra and stroked her long hair; Sandra's anger at seeing a gold chain round Agnes's ankle with the letters 'A. Lee McG' engraved on it; her irritation at having her dances with her father cut short so as not to exclude

---

Jungian painting 1
1969/70
71 x 56cm
Gouache on paper
No visible signature

SANDRA McGREGOR

I am indebted to John Scheepers and Father Manning who introduced me to Jungian Analysis. They both rejoiced at the completion of so successful an analysis. For me it was a miracle, God's work.

I destroyed all but four of my Jungian paintings, an action I subsequently regretted.

Agnes who sat out because, as Lee McGregor himself observed, "She does not know how to dance, her family were Quakers."

> *She's a Quaker, I thought and they consider dancing a sin. But break up a man's marriage and go all out to ensnare him – that is not a sin!*

What was at first jealousy and antagonism became bitter loathing between Sandra and Agnes.

Sandra visited her father in Somerset West each Sunday, at his request. Frequently, small but unpleasant incidents between Agnes and Sandra occurred, with Sandra invariably the loser. One Sunday a discussion on cookery led to Agnes fetching a large book. Sandra recognised it at once and the first thing she saw inside was her name, written in her own childish hand. She asked if she could take the book home with her.

"No," Agnes replied, "it's a book I use every day."

The following Sunday Sandra asked to see the book again. She opened it and found that the page with her name had been cut out. Sandra was afraid of Agnes and did not have the courage to tell her father. Doubtless he would not have believed her: in his eyes Agnes could do no wrong.

Sandra usually carried a basket rather than a handbag and it often contained, amongst other things, her precious notebook. Arriving at her father's house she left her basket inside while Agnes was making lunch. Sandra was sitting on the porch with her father. Later, when she looked in her basket the notebook was gone. Again, she did not have the courage to tell her father.

> *Before going to the station to return to Cape Town, I accused Agnes of taking my notebook. Agnes smiled sweetly and negated every word I said. As the train to Cape Town was drawing out my father stood looking at me and I at him, and his eyes never left mine. It is a long time ago now, but the bitter hatred I felt for Agnes is still there. From a life of joy and happiness, my life changed and became something dark.*

There were many similar incidents. Sandra felt from the start that Agnes intentionally set out to break the close relationship she had with her father. She learnt to hate Agnes, blaming her for everything, but still worshipping her father. She believed her father would never stop loving her. Similarly, Agnes hated Sandra. It was a distressing triangle. Alone with her father, he was the caring, wonderful person Sandra knew him to be, but Agnes made sure they were seldom left together on their own. This bitter relationship continued until her father's death in 1969.

CANON DAVID JENKINS, a priest at All Saints Church in Somerset West and a leading spiritual consultant, was a friend of Buck's. Sandra sought his help in 1965 having heard of his great gift of counselling and healing. She visited him by train twice a week on Tuesday and Thursday afternoons, for three years.

They met in his study and Sandra told him of her family, her home life, and her adoration of her father. She refused to accept that there was anything wrong in loving her father as she did. Sandra and David Jenkins spent many weeks unravelling the relationship, spiritually and psychologically.

Towards the end of this counselling, Sandra experienced a vision in David Jenkins' consulting room – one that would change her life. She suddenly became aware of a figure standing just behind David – an extraordinary empowering bright light which revealed a man with fair hair and very blue eyes, whose hands were raised in blessing.

I felt His presence and He has never left me.

Sandra told her father about her counselling, and that David Jenkins was initiating her into the Anglican Church. Her father was not interested. Her mother and brother were far away and communication with them was infrequent.

Sandra's family were not church-goers. Canon Jenkins felt that Sandra's whole life would change if she was confirmed, putting Jesus Christ at its centre. Sandra agreed. A delighted Dean King at St George's Cathedral in Cape Town, made arrangements for her confirmation.

It was July 1965, cold, pouring with rain. Sandra had no dresses or smart clothes. She wore heavy woollen stockings, her high black boots and her duffle coat from London. The service was to take place in the St John's Chapel. Sandra stood to the right of the altar, and the only other confirmation candidate, a young man dressed in a smart suit, stood to the left. Dean King, in his black cassock, came in first, leading in Bishop Philip Russell tap-tapping with his Bishop's crook. He smiled as he looked Sandra up and down, his eyes fixing on her black boots.

> *I could hear the rain on the roof and was surprised to hear knocking on the door. Only after the service did I find out it was Canon Jenkins who had come in from Somerset West on his motor-bike.*

After the service Sandra went straight back to District Six to get on with her painting – an interior fortunately.

It was understood that she would attend the 9.15am communion service at the Cathedral every Sunday. Sandra told her father that she would no longer be able to visit him on Sunday mornings. He was not pleased: he emphasised that he was her father, he came first in her life, he expected her on Sunday as usual, on time. This was possibly the first time that Sandra had the courage to oppose her father, but it still hurt her to have to refuse him. The matter was not mentioned again, and thereafter she visited him on Tuesdays. He had lost his total control over Sandra.

SANDRA PRAYED confidently to God for help, attending services at St George's Cathedral as she had promised, but never confessing her addiction. Despite her AA techniques and her increasing understanding of her problem, her prayers and cries for help were unanswered.

> *My bulimia continued but it did not interfere with my painting. Doctors I approached could not help my addiction, and I became increasingly desperate about it. I felt my life was filled with lies. In company I refused everything, especially sandwiches and cakes, asserting that I never ate them, and I was complimented on my willpower and my slim figure, but the deceit and cunning became increasingly intolerable.*

Ultimately, she confided in Father Liam Manning at St George's Cathedral in Cape Town. He advised her that there are two ways to reach God: through Holy Communion and the Sacraments, and through using one's gifts and talents, in her case, her art. He explained that the cause of addiction lies in the subconscious, which the conscious mind cannot reach, and that the subconscious mind can be reached and cleared by Jungian Analysis. Sandra knew Jungian Analysis would be expensive and could take two or three years – a solution beyond her means.

Fortunately Father Liam, himself a Jungian analyst, introduced her to John Scheepers, a retired therapist whose brother's life had been saved in an operation by Lee McGregor. Scheepers was also interested in art, which counted in Sandra's favour, and he shared Father Manning's view that art should be part of her therapy. He took on her case *pro bono*, and for two years John Scheepers became the centre of her life.

FROM THE BEGINNING, Scheepers insisted she draw and paint. Her art, her dreams and the analysis began to reveal the meaning of her addiction: the consequences of her indulged childhood, her obsession with her father, her jealousy and hatred of Agnes, and the influence of parental figures in her life. The therapy made it clear that in Jack Benoit, the elderly man she had loved in London, she saw her father in a sexual light.

> *Why those enormous binges of food? Why the particular cakes I needed? Why the cottage loaves and all that peanut butter? Why not marmalade or honey? Or bacon and eggs? Why the milky coffee I had to have? Why the binges of food and not brandy, whisky or gin? Why the choice of food with which I stuffed myself, why the purges? What did it mean?*

While working with Scheepers Sandra produced many paintings in gouache from her imagination, in which she explored and found the meaning of her life.

> *There in colour on enormous sheets of paper were the foods I ate and why I chose them, why I purged them. There it was. An extraordinary combination: AA, Anglicanism, Art, and Jung. It was a liberating experience, and it enabled me to control my addiction at last.*

At times the urges to eat returned, but they had lost their power. Sandra continued to use the short 'Jesus Prayer' – "Lord Jesus Christ, Son of God, have mercy on me, a sinner," and to live "just for today".

> Look to this day, for it is Life, the very life of Life.
> In its brief course lie all the verities and realities of your existence.
> The bliss of growth, the glory of action, the splendour of achievement
> Are but experiences of time.
> For yesterday is but a dream,
> And tomorrow only a vision;
> And today well lived makes yesterday a dream of happiness
> And tomorrow a vision of hope.
> Look well, therefore, to this day.

> *I never say I am completely cured: I say I am cured today.*

IT IS REMARKABLE how Sandra attracted people to help her when she most needed help: Buck gave her constant support for the first three years in Cape Town; Canon Jenkins, for three years; and her friend, Ray Querido, for over two years. Thereafter, it was John Scheepers, with whom Sandra underwent Jungian therapy for three years, and later there was Johann Strydom. He did not counsel Sandra, but was a constant, helpful and devoted friend for many years.

Each Saturday Sandra went to Ray Querido's flat at Mouille Point, where she painted 'fantasy' pictures. Possibly over a hundred such paintings. Ray would put out water, Sandra's paint brushes and a serving dish with

Jungian painting 2
1969/70
71 x 56cm
Gouache on paper
No visible signature

SANDRA McGREGOR

Sandra's gouache paints. Sandra just painted and pictures materialised as the paints ran into one another – a 'stream of consciousness' in colour.

She used only gouache, an opaque water colour paint which dries lighter than when wet. Sometimes she worked with candle wax on paper – using the candle to make wax marks which repel paint but adhere to the paper or board, to create a wonderful textured effect. Ray's therapy helped change Sandra's life.

SANDRA'S FATHER, during these years, led a retired life in Somerset West with Agnes, playing golf, collecting antiques, visiting Clarke's bookshop in Cape Town in search of Africana to add to his collection, doing some carpentry.

Agnes dominated him totally and seldom left Sandra alone with her father. Sandra found it impossible to discuss her work in District Six in Agnes's presence, so it became a closed subject and her father took little interest in what she was doing. Nor did he visit her in Cape Town. Their relationship changed but her love for him never wavered.

Sandra continued to paint in District Six, but knew her father would never understand her love for its coloured people.

Walking down Adderley Street one day I saw an elderly coloured lady struggling with a large, heavy suitcase. I carried it for her, unaware that my father and Agnes were in Cape Town for the day and had seen me. My father thought it a very strange thing to do. Agnes had a good deal to say, but somehow I did not care quite so much.

Agnes told Sandra nothing of her father's health. One day, when she was visiting her father in Somerset West, he told her that he had been having trouble with the veins in his legs: he would he going into Groote Schuur the following week. Agnes would stay at a hotel near the hospital. He added that Sandra should not visit him until a week after the operation.

When, on a previous visit to Groote Schuur for tests, Sandra had visited him. The Ward Sister told her that Mrs McGregor had refused to leave her husband and had spent the night in an adjoining ward, something normally never allowed. "I must disillusion you, Sister," Sandra had replied. "Mrs McGregor is my mother, and she is not here."

When Lee McGregor entered Groote Schuur, the second time, Sandra went to see him before the operation. Agnes was there of course, holding his hands. Sandra tried to tell him of her love for him, but with Agnes sitting there it was impossible.

> *When I got up to go, he followed me out. I stood in his arms and he held me tight – then he said, "Kiss me again." I did so, and burst into tears, and walked away, crying bitterly, watched by a coloured man standing nearby.*

The next day her father had the operation. Although Sandra had agreed not to visit him until the following week, something made her go to the hospital. A Sister, who saw Sandra about to enter the small private ward, said she must be very careful not to upset the patient.

> *I did not know what she meant. I went in and there stood 'that woman', bending over my father and clasping both his hands. He had tubes everywhere. He seemed aware of my presence and tried to smile. Agnes looked at me and told me to leave, adding that my father did not even know I was there.*
>
> *I hesitated for a moment – and then he gave such a big sigh and said, "I am so tired." I took away with me his awareness of my presence and the slight smile that had passed over his face.*

LEE MCGREGOR DIED on the 7 June 1969, a few months before his 75th birthday. Davy came down from the farm for the funeral, and he and Sandra sat together for the service. Their mother wanted to be there with them. She was, in fact, still Lee McGregor's wife, she still loved him and had never agreed to divorce him. Agnes, who was no doubt distressed, made it clear she did not want Florence there.

Glowing obituaries appeared in the press, praising Lee McGregor for the devoted years he had given to the medical profession, and his dedication to the highest standards of surgery. It was reported that the 1969 edition of his book, *Synopsis of Surgical Anatomy*, first published in 1932, had been revised to his satisfaction just two months before his death.

Florence outlived him by seven years. Towards the end of her life, after several falls she required constant care and was moved from the farm to Nazareth House in Kimberley, an establishment which cared for those in need. She remained there for two years. A remarkable Irish nun, Sister Finbarr, treated Florence as if she were her own mother, being immensely loving and kind towards her. Florence was happy there.

In 1976 Sandra received word that that she should go to her mother as soon as possible. Julian and Joyce Adler booked her on a plane immediately and took her to the airport. Sandra was able to spend a few days with her mother. Towards the end, the Mother Superior sat in the ward reading the

Bible. The Dean of Kimberley, Tom Stannich, administered the sacraments, gave Florence Holy Communion, and a few hours later she died quietly. It was a blessed experience for Sandra.

> *Suddenly my mother's whole face was illumined with the gold of Christ – all the lines left her face and she looked young again. Everything was golden for about five minutes, then all gradually faded.*

CHAPTER 13

My friends the 'skollies'

On 11 February 1966, District Six was finally declared a 'white area' under the Group Areas Act of 1950. The Nationalist Government planned to evict the inhabitants, raze the buildings and redevelop the area for whites.

This move had been expected, and by the time of this declaration many of the better-off families were beginning to leave. The whole area, with most of the buildings owned by absentee landlords, was already dilapidated. It deteriorated even more as owners abandoned any maintenance of properties. By 1968 the process of forced removals had begun. It took until 1982 to flatten and clear the area, and some 60,000 residents were sent to distant and desolate regions of the Cape Flats. Only the mosques and churches remained.

The destroyed District came to represent the enormous injustice of white domination and had far-reaching implications for the political history of South Africa. The eviction of this cosmopolitan community whose families had been living in District Six for generations, reverberated throughout South Africa and beyond. The rage it caused halted any renewal plans by the government and to this day there are still large areas of the District left untouched.

Sandra witnessed the destruction of this vibrant society and its effect on the people of the District with great distress. Nevertheless, she continued to record life in the District as it was gradually destroyed, reflecting what remained of its warmth and cheerfulness, and depicting its pain and impending tragedy. These were fruitful years of dedication during which she produced remarkable work. Sandra showed courageous concern for those she had grown to love in this community which had virtually brought her back to life, and to which she owed so much.

AS WORD OF THE QUEST for Sandra's work slowly spread, information trickled in. Julian Adler advised where some of these paintings could be found. He had sold many on Sandra's behalf and had collected her work himself. Four paintings belong to his daughter Cindy, who took them to America; others are still held locally – Sea Point, Camps Bay, Newlands, Pinelands, and Kenilworth. Sandra's excitement on seeing her work again, after some forty years, made the search rewarding and motivated the whole project. Gradually, the extent of her work began to emerge more clearly.

Mr Lewis' second-hand shop in Caledon Street
1966
46 x 35cm
Pen, sepia ink and gouache
Signed bottom right

CINDY YEOMAN

One of the two men sitting outside the shop, the man nearest the door, Gelaggies, was a familiar figure in Cape Town. He had a limp and walked with difficulty, a crutch under one arm and often a sack over his other shoulder. The man in the red jersey and blue jeans, standing with one foot on the pavement, is Claude, whom I knew quite well.

I painted a cross in almost every painting – there is one in the lower pane of the upstairs sash window, grey against a yellow background.

Sandra McGregor – 'Onse artist' in District Six

Balcony scene

Late 1960s
36 x 46cm
Pen, sepia ink and gouache
Signed top left

CINDY YEOMAN

Built in 1900 this building was typical of many in District Six with people living upstairs and shops below. The balconies were communal and good places for meeting and gossiping.

My friends the 'skollies'

Hanover Lane and Big Sophie

Late 1960s
33 x 45cm
Pen, sepia ink and gouache
Signed bottom right

There were many steep lanes in the District and I painted several of them at different times. Big Sophie is about to go down Hanover Lane. The 'skollies' on the right have their flagon of wine.

PRIVATE COLLECTION

Sandra McGregor – 'Onse artist' in District Six

Hanover Lane scene with chicken

Late 1960s
35 x 45cm
Pen, sepia ink and gouache
Signed top left

In this similar scene a man has passed out on the pavement and drinking has started in earnest.

CINDY YEOMAN

The Seven Steps – woman with curlers, is one of Cindy Yeoman's four paintings in Los Angeles. The other three are *Mr. Lewis' second-hand shop in Caledon Street, Balcony scene*, and *Hanover Lane scene with chicken*.

Sandra painted *Mr. Lewis' second-hand shop in Caledon Street* in 1966, when life was still relatively normal in District Six. This building was a landmark. Solid and well built, the intricately carved wooden brackets supporting the verandah roof gave it an old-fashioned air of elegance. As usual, Sandra incorporated people loitering in the streets.

Interesting buildings always caught Sandra's eye, as did street scenes. There was an old building, on the corner of Hanover Street and Lavender Hill, typical of many buildings, with shops on street level and flats above. A communal balcony ran in front of the flats.

Big Sophie was a character, full of fun, part of the general crowd. Children teased her because of her size. Sandra painted her about to enter Hanover Lane, a passageway from Caledon Street down to the Seven Steps. *Hanover Lane scene with chicken* is a similar scene to the previous work, but is later in the day – again, life as lived in the street.

IN DECEMBER 2007 Julian Adler sent an email regarding an unrecorded Sandra McGregor work he had found:

> In one shop I had noticed a pile of pictures propped up against each other and edging out of the pile saw enough colour palette to recognize the work of our friend Sandra. Flipped three other no-goods forward and there in full view *The Dairy* painting!
>
> Julian

This painting was of the Rose & Crown Dairy in Hanover Street, opposite a lane called Rotten Row. Sandra would have painted this scene in the dying days of the District. Normally this corner would be bustling with people. The old Malay man and his grandchild seem singularly alone.

Sandra had painted Rotten Row previously, before the demolition had begun, but she has no record of the painting.

> *I remember there were two 'skollies', and the girl-friend of one of them wore a very short bright pink dress and blue curlers in her hair. The 'skollies', as usual, were in their uniform of jeans and bright sweaters. I also recall a deep purple shadow on the wall of the lane, which added a sense of drama to the scene.*

Sandra McGregor – 'Onse artist' in District Six

Rose & Crown Dairy
1970s
51 x 41cm
Pen, ink and gouache
Signed bottom right

JULIAN ADLER

Businesses were closing and people leaving, but there was still so much to draw and paint. There are still living quarters above the dairy but the timber in the cart will be used to board up the windows prior to eviction.

I liked the tragic emptiness of this scene. It was almost as if the old man and the boy were intruders.

Julian, and his late wife Joyce, were close to Sandra and she was grateful for all that he did for her in those days, when she was very much in need of friendship and support.

HORSBURG LANE painted in 1967, also ran between Caledon and Hanover streets, and descended steeply to Waynicks, a well-known dress shop at the bottom of the lane.

On this corner at the top of the lane, Gillie, Ernie and Bernie often gathered with their friends. Sometimes they were joined by Doos, a much older man. Each of these men Sandra came to know well. Gillie was sometimes with the group, sometimes not, as he was often in gaol for selling drugs; no sooner was he out of prison than he'd be selling again. It was a tough world for the 'skollies'. They were always getting into some kind of trouble. One day Bernie was stabbed in the thigh and asked Sandra to help him. He was too afraid to go to hospital. Sandra explained the position to the chemist who sold her a Red Cross kit to dress a superficial knife wound. She returned to Bernie, and surrounded by his friends in a dark room, lit only by a single lamp, she did what she could. The wound healed beautifully and Bernie was always grateful. More than once he asked Sandra to dress his wounds.

Once there was a fight between Gillie and Ernie in Motjie Ragmat's yard. Ernie was stabbed just below the eye and there was blood everywhere. Subsequently I visited Ernie in Groote Schuur Hospital, an action unheard of for a white woman. I also met his young son at the hospital who resembled his father absolutely. Ernie was sitting up in bed, looking extraordinarily clean – the hospital had given him a bath. He seemed very shy when he saw me.

The following day, in the late afternoon, Sandra walked higher up Hanover Street than before. It was nearly dark and she saw a circle of men around a perforated drum of burning coals. As she walked slowly towards this gang, she sensed not friendliness as in Caledon Street, but hostility. A man moved, put something in his coat pocket and walked slowly towards her.

Sandra always carried her basket of paint brushes and wore a cross. She greeted one of them and when there was no response, said, "Do you know Gillie and Ernie and Bernie in Caledon Street?"

"Oh," said the leader, looking at her paintbrushes, "Jy het Ernie in hospitaal gevisit – jy is die artist?"

Horsburg Lane
1967
57 x 45cm
Pen, sepia ink and gouache
No visible signature

CHRIS AND MIKE BROWN

In the distance the docks are visible where many of the men of the District worked, often as casual labour. Gillie is the tall man side-on to the viewer, Bernie stands in the doorway, Ernie wears a hat and sits on the pavement. This painting was sold for R15 in 1967.

From that moment they were friendly – the grapevine was at work everywhere in the District. She saw this gang of 'skollies' quite often, and painted many of them, in their jeans and studded black belts.

DOOS WAS FREQUENTLY SEEN in Caledon Street, near this corner where Ernie and his friends gathered. One day after a fight, Doos asked Sandra to help him. Motjie Ragmat was angry and insisted on being present and would not let her be alone with Doos. Only years later did Sandra learn that Doos had been arrested by the police and given a lengthy sentence. He had escaped from prison and continued living in District Six. Everyone knew this, but no-one gave him away: such was the code of the District.

One Saturday afternoon Sandra saw Doos sitting on the pavement, his back against a wall. As soon as he saw her he started to sing the traditional 'klopse' songs that she loved. Sandra listened for a while, then waved and said goodbye and walked home. The next day she was told by the children that Doos, who was often inebriated, had been arrested for drunkenness. He was locked up in a cell in Caledon Square with another man who had been in Worcester prison with Doos years before. This man betrayed Doos to the police.

On the day Doos came up for trial, Sandra went to the courtroom. She found herself the only person on the designated 'Whites Only' side: a group of coloured people sat in a separate area on the other side. After several prisoners were led up from the cells to plead their cases, Doos was at last led up, in chains. This was the first time Sandra had ever seen a man in chains.

Doos stood in the dock. He looked slowly at the coloured people present, and then looked at the 'Whites Only' side. With a start he recognised me – he gave me a look of such gratitude and wonderment.

It was Sandra's practice during all these years to carry a crucifix in the pocket of her jeans. Sitting in the court, she saw that a young Afrikaans policeman was in charge of Doos. Quietly she attracted the attention of the policeman and asked him if he would give her crucifix to Doos. This he promised to do. Before he led Doos down the steps to the cells, he allowed him to stop for a moment and look at Sandra again. It was a look which has Sandra has never forgotten. Doos was given fifteen years.

Many years later, Sandra was painting on the field which ended at Caledon Street when some children came racing up to her, crying, "Miss artist, Doos is uit. Doos is uit." It was the same Doos, but fifteen years older, with the same old grey hat to hide his white hair.

SANDRA LEARNT a lot about these men, and in 1968 wrote a letter to the Cape Times defending them:

MY FRIENDS THE 'SKOLLIES'
From Miss SANDRA McGREGOR (Cape Town)
Among the many friends I have in District Six are men labelled "skollies" or even "gangsters"!
… May I suggest sympathy and compassion replace judgment and censure …
… Instead of condemning them, rather seek to understand the frustrations, the indignities, the deep underlying problems.

I have painted many 'skollies' and how much they teach me of life and of courage! Vital, dynamic characters, colourfully dressed, they are splendid models – with a natural gift for rhythm and exciting, graceful movement.

How much do I as an artist owe to these men – to their love of life, their kindness and courtesy, their sense of humour and the fellowship with which they enter into my pictures! Lastly, they are my guardians and protectors, so that I can paint anywhere in District Six.

One Saturday afternoon, Sandra decided to paint a scene at the lower end of Hanover Street. It was a lovely summer's day. The District appeared to be deserted, most people having gone to the beach. She sat on the pavement in front of an old building where a group of 'skollies' loitered – well supplied with wine for the afternoon. Sandra asked if she could paint them and, as always, they were delighted. After a while, around the corner came two women and a little child. They looked surprised to see Sandra painting, and came and stood behind her, interested in what she was doing.

The 'skollies', seeing Sandra had an audience, decided to come across and see her painting too. At that, one of the women said, "Ma, wat doen al die 'skollies'? Kom – ons moet gaan – ons wil nie trouble hê nie!"

The other woman laughed and said, "Weet jy nie wie die vrou is? Sy's die moeder van al die 'skollies' in District Six."

ONE DAY SANDRA walked halfway up Clifton Street which ran beyond St Mark's Church. It was the hour when the children returned home from school. She sat outside Ernie's mother's house, admiring the view, stretching as far as Waynicks in Hanover Street and the docks. On her left was the field with the beautiful tree – and the Seven Steps beyond that. The field stretched right down to Caledon Street.

Sandra painted this field on Clifton Street twice, once with a boy with a bicycle in the foreground and another time when the Group Areas demolition was in progress. In the first painting *The Field with bicycle boy*, scenes of busy life and much activity are visible in the field below the tree.

The young man in the foreground was supposed to be delivering goods higher up Clifton Street, but at Sandra's request he posed beside his bicycle and, of course, the children came running to be in the painting too, and stayed until late watching Sandra.

"*Draw my af, Miss Sandera, draw my af.*" Words that echo in my heart.

In the second painting, *The Field with truck*, the field is emptier, and men on the far roof are dismantling the corrugated iron sheeting prior to the demolition of those houses.

The entire scene in both paintings is dominated by the skyline of Cape Town and by the tree on the field in the foreground. This tree, too, was later bulldozed, and only a stump remained as testimony to a once vibrant community.

> *I never passed the open fields in Caledon Street without remembering the laughter and the gaiety and the joie de vivre. At some later date a film was made of the empty fields and the empty Bloemhof Flats and Stirling Flats, with shattered windows ... But across the bare fields and through the broken windows, came the voices of children at play, and the voices of the women of District Six, laughing and talking, shouting, singing as they always used to do.*

THE ONSLAUGHT of the demolition of District Six began in earnest in the late sixties, when the bulldozers and front-end loaders increased the pace of their work. Sandra remembers being in a house in Tennant Street, when a white man with papers in his hands knocked at the door. The family hid behind the curtains, refusing to open the door, dreading the eviction news he would bring. Official letters, in buff envelopes, were then posted to each house: the recipients were to report in person to Barrack Street with proof of identity and racial group.

> *Many of my friends went on as usual, refusing to face the tragedy that lay ahead.*

Sandra McGregor – 'Onse artist' in District Six

The Field with bicycle boy
1968/9
Approx. 51 x 61cm
Pen, sepia ink and gouache
No visible signature

OWNER UNKNOWN

People are still living in the adjacent houses, washing is still hanging out, and the cyclist and three school children are watching me paint.

The Field with truck

1968/9
51 x 61cm
Pen, ink and gouache
No visible signature

OWNER UNKNOWN

Demolition men are dismantling a corrugated iron roof and a truck is being loaded with rubble. The men around the table are playing 'Kerim', a game played on a table with a ball and long sticks. The bicycle boy has gone. The wood collected by the boys would have been found in and around the demolished buildings and burned for heating. The steps at the end of the field led down to the Seven Steps and Hanover Street.

Sandra McGregor – 'Onse artist' in District Six

156

National Cinema at night
1970s
56 x 43cm
Pen, ink and gouache
Signed bottom right

PRIVATE COLLECTION

I consider this the most exciting painting I did of the National, and doubt if anyone else ever painted the interior. Bob, the doorman is leaning against the entrance door. One of the DKs, he was older than most of them, medium height, and expressive dark eyes. After the National *burnt down, Bob sold* The Argus *on the Parade, until he died of a heart attack some months later.*

In the box office is Bones, so called because he was small and thin. It was winter and Bones wore his blue balaclava. He was always kind to me and I was upset to hear of his death a few months later after he was stabbed in a gang fight.

Standing on the stairs, is Maantjie, a dramatic figure, with light skin and blue-grey eyes and one of the leaders of the DKs. The blue jeans, white shirt, amulet round his neck, sheepskin jacket with fur collar, and the heavy studded black belt typify the gang leader. Maantjie died in 2003, aged fifty-nine.

SANDRA HAD BEEN INSIDE the National Cinema from time to time and she was determined to paint the foyer by night, with its mysterious shadows and bright lights. She chose the stairs going up to the first floor — a splendid composition of perspective and of light and dark — and knew it would be a challenge in drawing and painting. She produced the basic drawing sitting in the foyer during the day. The stairs were worn by the feet of years of opera-goers, and those of thousands of people who packed the cinemas. The three characters in this painting, Bob, Bones and Maantjie, were asked to pose and Sandra knew them all well.

Everybody who entered the National saw Sandra drawing, smiled and greeted her. There were no women at these film shows, and the cinema teemed with 'skollies'. At the interval they poured out and crowded around her pushing and pulling in order to see the painting. Mr Faber, in his thirties, ran the British and the National after his father became too old. Afraid for Sandra's safety, he stood watching, holding a revolver hidden in his coat pocket. Sandra knew the 'skollies' would never harm her.

I wish I could express in words what I captured in this painting: the atmosphere, excitement and possible danger of the National by night. The golden light and the dark purple shadows. The mounting tension and drama. It is as if all three figures were looking directly at me.

SANDRA WITNESSED many fights in the District, fights with fists, knives, bottles, pangas, but never firearms. One Saturday afternoon Sandra had been warned by Motjie Ragmat to go home early as there had been a lot of drinking on the street. The next morning Motjie Ragmat told Sandra that shortly after she had packed up her things and left, there was a fight on the very field where she had been painting. A gang had been drinking heavily and their leader, Broertjie, had stabbed a rival gang member to death. Broertjie had fled to his grandmother's room to hide. In vehicles and on foot, the opposing gang had sought him out, shouting his name. Realising they would find him sooner or later, he had given himself up to the police.

After Broertjie's trial, he was sentenced and held in Pollsmoor Prison, a maximum security prison situated in Tokai in the Constantiaberg Valley. Nelson Mandela, South Africa's most famous prisoner, was moved to this prison from Robben Island in 1982.

Sandra decided to go to Pollsmoor and take Broertjie some cigarettes. She had no idea how to get there, but was told to go by train to Mowbray station and then take the Pollsmoor bus. At Mowbray, she saw a group of

Sandra McGregor – 'Onse artist' in District Six

St Mark's Church

Late 1960s
51 x 59cm
Pen and ink and gouache
No visible signature

CHRIS AND MIKE BROWN

St Mark's off Caledon Street, looked directly on to the docks below. The cars are parked at an angle towards the pavement so that they would not roll down the steep hill. I often saw children collecting wood not just for heating in winter but also for cooking.

> *I used to sit at a front table, looking on to the street, so that I could see the vans bringing prisoners to the Supreme Court. One afternoon the Pollsmoor van arrived, and I saw the faces of prisoners peering through the bars. In these old vans, one could see the hands that clutched the bars, and the eyes of some of the men.*
>
> *Something impelled me to walk close to the prison van and hold up my cruficix for them to see – and a man's voice cried out. "Dis onse artist! Dis onse artist!"*
>
> *The driver of the van ordered me to go away – but he could not diminish the warmth, acceptance and acknowledgement of my place in their District.*

Sandra was sometimes invited to wonderful Greek parties at Nick's home in Sea Point: roast lamb over a grill, delicious Greek salads and rich cakes; parties breaking up at three in the morning. When their beloved daughter died, their grief was such that she seldom went to their restaurant, and in due course they moved away.

◆

> "No," I said, "I am not. I am sunburned from painting all day in District Six. It is obviously dangerous in South Africa to have a tan."

At that the officer apologised for the rudeness of his juniors, and asked Sandra what had brought her to Pollsmoor and whom she had come to see. Sandra told him about Broertjie and he told her to find out his name and number and return on Thursday. He promised that he would personally escort her to the prisoner.

THURSDAY CAME, and armed with Broertjie's surname and number, Sandra once again caught the train and bus to Pollsmoor. The same women walked with her and she wished them good luck as she entered the 'WHITES ONLY' office.

Sandra was met by the same officer He gave her a clean towel and soap to wash her hands, and then suggested she sit down and relax after the long journey. A short time later he led her to see Broertjie. The officer told Sandra to stand opposite Broertjie, behind a thick glass partition. Sandra spoke to Broertjie about the picture he had seen her painting, and gave him greetings from his family and friends.

> The Broertjie I knew was tall and well built and a real 'gang leader': the Broertjie I saw in the prison yard (he was there alone) was young and frightened and afraid.
>
> Then I showed him the little crucifix I always carried in the pocket of my jeans. He stood there crying, and I reminded him that God was with him, he wasn't alone. I became aware of several police officers standing around me, watching and listening to every word.

It was time to go. They led Broertjie away, and escorted Sandra back to the front office. One of the warders asked her why she had come to see a coloured man in prison: they were all surprised that a white woman would care about a coloured gangster. Sandra replied that she had painted many 'skollies' in District Six, that they were her friends and their welfare was a matter of concern for her.

"Your friends?" he sneered. "They are pigs! Be alone with them in the police cells and they would stab you in the back without a second thought."

IN KEEROM STREET, opposite the Supreme Court, Nick, a Greek, and his wife owned an excellent restaurant, The Court Lounge. Nick was a marvellous cook and he served splendid meals for low prices.

A lane between Caledon and Hanover Streets
1960s
Approx. 57 x 45cm
Pen, ink and raw sienna
No visible signature

OWNER UNKNOWN

This is one of my earliest paintings of the District. I was experimenting with colour, using pen and ink and raw sienna, and using many people in the scene. There are several children in the foreground watching me paint.

There were many small lanes, such as this one, between these two streets. The painting was done in the evening light.

coloured women, some of whom were elderly, standing together, holding parcels and carrier bags, and she joined them.

At last the bus arrived. They rattled along a dusty road and ultimately turned into the prison grounds. Sandra did not know where to go, but one of the women said to her, "Go there – where it says 'WHITES ONLY'". Sandra entered an office where a policeman sat at a desk. She told him she had come to see a prisoner and asked him where she should go. In those days Sandra was burnt brown by working long hours in the sun. Impatiently the man said, "Up there. You don't come in here."

She walked 'up there', joining her fellow bus passengers. It was a very hot summer's day, and by the time they reached a gate where they were to wait, the older women sank to the dusty ground in exhaustion. There were no seats nor shelter of any kind. Sandra noticed a building behind this gate, which had barred windows, and to her astonishment, she saw hands waving at her, and heard shouts of, "Miss artist, Miss artist."

Sandra told the women she had come to see Broertjie, and they asked, "Wat is sy van? What is his surname and what is his number?" Sandra had no idea. She noticed a policeman who, scowling, put a table into position and rattled a key in the large lock of the gate. The women immediately formed a queue, and kindly let Sandra in near the front. It was almost four o'clock. They had been standing waiting for two hours. One of the women said to Sandra, "He's calling you." Sandra, realised the policeman was shouting at her.

I looked directly at him, and saw only immense hatred in his eyes. I have never forgotten that look. When I asked to see Broertjie, but could not give his surname or number, the policeman became so offensive that I began to walk away. At the same time he shouted that it was four o'clock, their time was up, and they would all have to come back on Thursday. Looking up to the windows of the building again, I saw hands holding on to the bars, and a voice called out again, "Miss artist, onse artist."

Slowly the women gathered up their belongings and began to walk in the direction of the bus stop. Sandra walked with them. She left them to go into the office marked 'WHITES ONLY'.

This time, the same policeman was still at his desk but an officer was also present. I told him that never in all my life had I experienced the insolence, rudeness and abuse that the policeman at the gate had hurled at me. The officer said carefully, "Excuse me, are you not coloured?"

CHAPTER 14

The wrecking ball

Sandra sat on empty fields painting the shops and buildings that remained. The bulldozers worked on either side of her. The dust was suffocating, the noise deafening, as building after building came down. Churches and mosques were left untouched. Religion continued to play a vital role in the dwindling community life in District Six.

In the late 1960s, Sandra painted St Mark's Church, in pen and ink and gouache, as it stood proudly in what was becoming a ravaged landscape. Many houses and shops had been torn down, but the small houses at the side of the church in Clifton Street were still standing.

In 1865 the Foundation Stone of the school chapel of St Mark the Evangelist was laid by Bishop Gray, but the building soon proved too small. The growth of the District brought the need for a larger church building. In 1887, the present St Mark's was built on Clifton Hill, using sandstone from Table Mountain, and imported stained glass. The Foundation Stone was laid by the Governor, Sir Hercules Robinson and the church was named St Mark's-on-the-Hill.

Reverend John da Costa, the priest who looked after St Marks, became a famous figure in District Six. He was a colourful, strong, no-nonsense character – and a friend of Sandra's. Born in the East End of London, he was a huge man, well used to dealing with fights in the streets. He established a gym in one of the buildings, and taught schoolboys and others to box. On Sundays the boys and girls in his Church Brigade marched from St Mark's through the streets of the District, with bugles blaring, drums beating and flags flying. Father John da Costa was proud of his Brigade, and loved to hear the crowd cheering. He was dedicated to District Six and all her people.

Sandra painted a portrait of John da Costa. A photograph of Sandra at work appeared in The Argus on 28 May 1970.

> CAPE TOWN artist, Sandra McGregor, has painted a portrait of
> Rev. John da Costa, known to many as the 'fighting priest of
> District Six' for the tough way in which he has dealt with skollies
> in the area. Here, Sandra McGregor puts the finishing touches to
> her painting, while Father da Costa dutifully poses.

He was a brave man, whose courage the 'skollies' admired because he was fearless. When gangs were fighting he would get into the centre of the fight, and disarm the leaders. In his rectory he had a variety of weapons collected through the years.

One hot summer afternoon, Sandra had been painting all day in Ayre Street. Children helped carry her easel and art equipment to Motjie Ragmat's house. Suddenly Sandra heard blood-curdling screams coming from a house across the road. Immediately a crowd gathered, and someone phoned the police.

It transpired that a man with a cut-throat razor was chasing a woman in the house. No one dared go to her assistance. Two police cars arrived and parked just outside the house, but the policemen were afraid to leave their cars. The police had guns but nobody moved. A child next to Sandra said that Father John was in the house.

The screaming stopped and out of the house came Father John, holding a scruffy-looking individual by the neck. He held up the cut-throat razor to add to his collection – and laughingly signalled to the police, shouting, "Kom! Kom! Nou kan julle uitklim!" Slowly, one by one, the policemen climbed out of their cars, guns and all.

Father John's rectory was in Caledon Street and when invited to dinner Sandra saw another side of this giant of a man. He set a candlelit table and soft music played in the background. He loved good music and had a wide collection of classical music on tape. He refused to allow anyone to help as he served a delicious three-course meal he had made for his guests. His mother had been a cook in London – and no doubt he had learnt his considerable culinary skills from her. After the meal came coffee and music. The pavement outside was deserted when Sandra left, save for three men stretched out on the paving stones, the ubiquitous flagon of wine nearby, and a thin dog scrounging in a dustbin.

After many years as the priest of St Mark's, Father John was sent to Johannesburg, and then to Rhodesia as Dean of Salisbury. He took the memorial service held after a Viscount airliner civilian plane was shot down shortly after take-off from Kariba, by an anti-aircraft rocket fired by Joshua Nkomo's Zimbabwe Peoples Revolution Army (ZIPRA). Only eighteen of fifty-six passengers aboard survived the crash and crawled out of the wreckage. Ten of these survivors were subsequently murdered by ZIPRA 'terrorists' at the crash site.

Dean John da Costa preached at the Memorial Service for victims of this horrific event. His passionate and memorable sermon, 'A Deafening Silence', accused nations, which called themselves civilized, of remaining mute.

The sermon was taped and 25 000 copies of it were sold around the world. Bishop Desmond Tutu was one of the few who strongly condemned this killing, but the Dean was bitterly criticised by the Rhodesian government and he was subsequently deported.

John da Costa took his portrait with him when he left for London, and died of cancer some years later. The whereabouts of the portrait, painted in oil, is unknown, and Sandra has no photograph of it.

SANDRA ALSO PAINTED the Muir Street Mosque, the biggest of the four District Six mosques. It is an imposing edifice in a Spanish-Moorish style, with two towers and a 75 foot high minaret from which prayers were broadcast. There is no record of this painting either, and its whereabouts is unknown.

Muslim men in the District were strict about their religion. They attended prayers, feasts and ceremonies regularly, always wearing prayer-caps of white crochet or other material. Their children were required to attend madrasah – a religious school – each afternoon after school, and boys and girls were obliged to wear white head coverings.

At the madrasah they learnt the fundamentals of Arabic, Islamic history, and passages from the Koran. In this way they preserved a Cape tradition going back to the days of Simon van der Stel, when their ancestors arrived at the Cape as political exiles or slaves from countries like Malaya.

Muslim children on their way to the madrasah.

There were no vacations for the children. During the public school holidays madrasah classes were held in the mornings. Even in the dying days of the District, with many of the buildings reduced to rubble, this teaching continued – and the children continued to dress accordingly.

Muslims, Christians, Jews and Hindus lived together harmoniously in the District for generations. In Aspeling Street the Ebenezer Dutch Reformed Mission Church stood right next to the Aspeling Street Mosque. Clifton Street is long since gone and St Mark's Anglican Church is now surrounded by the modern grey concrete buildings of the Cape Peninsula University of Technology. Congregants – many of them older people who remember what it was to hold an eviction notice in their hands – still travel from outlying districts, mostly the Cape Flats, to worship at St Mark's on Sundays. In July 2008, the announcement that this historic church was to undergo a R1.8 million renovation was greeted with joy by many.

ON 28 JUNE 1968, an article entitled DESPAIR SEEN IN DISTRICT SIX, was published in the Argus, and a longer version, DISTRICT SIX IS A DESPAIRING, DYING WORLD, appeared on 29 June:

> 'There is an air of utter hopelessness and despair in District Six,' says Miss Sandra Mc Gregor…
>
> … 'When I first started painting District Six, there was just a fire, a love of living – it was all an exciting way of life. There was a lot of joy.
>
> … 'Today it's like painting a dying world … a destroyed soul. There is still a lot of laughter there, but if one looks below the surface, one finds only misery and sickness …'

IN THE GALANSKY BUILDING in Hanover Street, there were two well-known shops which stood side by side – Vasson's Shoe Repairs and Boete Leiman's Fruit and Vegetable Shop. Sandra painted them both when they were among the last shops still standing. All buildings on the other side of the road had already been knocked down, leaving a bare, untidy field.

The Vassons were first class shoemakers and Sandra always took her shoes to them to be repaired. Gopal Vasson came to Cape Town as a young married man, with one child, a son named Dalpit. They came from Kadod, a village in the state of Gujerat, India. Gopal set up shop in Sea Point, later moved to Alma Road, Rosebank, then to Kloof Street and subsequently to Somerset Road, each time opening a shop and shoe repair service. Finally, he opened the shop at 172 Hanover Street in District Six.

The wrecking ball

Vasson's Shoe Shop

Late 1970s
41 x 51cm
Pen, ink and gouache
No visible signature

PRIVATE COLLECTION

One of the last shops still standing, I painted this sitting in a dusty, rubble-strewn field across the road. Mr Vasson is working behind his counter while a small boy watches him. Pavements were places to gather and to play, even during the demolition.

Boete Leiman's Fruit and Vegetable Shop

Late 1970s
Approx 41 x 51cm
Pen, sepia ink and gouache
Signed bottom left

MANUELA ZUIDEMA

Boete Leiman is leaning against the pillar on the right while his brother poses in the doorway for me. On the left is Arundel Street. I had to tell the little boy sitting on the pavement, "Don't move, I am painting you!" Dr Behardien's consulting rooms are on the left of the building and are closed. Sheets of corrugated iron have been nailed over the windows. On the far right is Mr Vasson's shoe shop, also closed up. The District was dying.

Sandra's painting of Vasson's shoe shop shows the effect of the demolitions. The windows already have strong wire mesh screening across them. Next door, Hanover Barber had been closed up for good. There were wire-netting screens across the whole front of this shop.

This painting was sold many years ago to a Cape Town couple who still own it. I took Sandra to see it and she was overjoyed. She had not seen it since she painted it.

Sandra met Gopal's grandson, Vinod Vasson, in 2004. Their joy at seeing each other after so many years was clearly evident. Vinod talked of his upbringing in District Six and recalled watching Sandra painting, seated in this uneven field facing the row of shops, with Table Mountain towering behind. Some days, after rain, Sandra walked over the mud to set up her easel. Then Vinod and others would run out to put newspapers down on the ground so that she would not get her feet wet.

Boete Leiman's Fruit and Vegetable Shop, next door to Vasson's, was one of the last shops Sandra painted. The houses on the opposite side of the street no longer existed. Boete Leiman traded in the Galansky Building, but like his neighbours he did not own his shop.

With the threat of the Group Areas Act hanging over them, owners of shops in District Six stopped repairing or maintaining their properties.

Kind residents would lend Sandra two chairs – one to sit on and one as an easel – which the children carried for her. Sometimes their mothers would give Sandra sweet tea or a cold drink.

Consequently the area deteriorated into a virtual slum. The District, though, still bustled with activity. Sandra knew, like everyone else, that time was running out: she was determined to capture the vibrancy of a community of which she had become part.

> *This painting was completed a week before the shop itself was bulldozed. I had spent six weeks on this painting, hours and hours every day, so when the bulldozers and front-end loaders moved in part of me died with that building as it was torn apart.*
>
> *They came with machinery and a great iron ball and demolished it completely. I stood on the field watching. It was like the murder of something I loved. My heart was breaking.*

When he was about nine years old, Fareed Rossier was sent to buy food at Boete Leiman's Fruit and Vegetable Shop not long before it was demolished. When he got there, Sandra was painting the shop and, as always, he was fascinated. He forgot his shopping and returned home late, empty handed, to be given a hiding. In the afternoon after school, Fareed used to follow Sandra and would watch her drawing and painting. Her drawing inspired him and he began to draw on the pavements with chalk.

Fareed's father was a plasterer and the family were contented living in District Six, until obliged to leave. Removal day came ten days before

The boy watching Sandra paint Boete Leiman's Fruit and Vegetable Shop is Fareed Rossier.

Fareed's eighteenth birthday, 11 October 1980, and Fareed vividly described their departure: he was upset that day and remembers clearly sitting on a truck piled with their belongings. A bulldozer idled next to the family house which was about to be demolished. In anger he threw a brick at the driver. He saw the bulldozer start its destructive work, and he watched their house go down. He cried, and his mother cried as they were driven away. Later he realised he had forgotten an iron horse on wheels in the cellar. It had belonged to his grandmother.

He never went to art school nor had formal lessons, but he has been practising as an artist ever since. He taught himself to work in oil, charcoal, pastel and watercolour.

DARKNESS WAS FALLING OVER DISTRICT Six, yet Sandra still went every day to sketch or paint.

Much of this work I did then is lost: Oxford Place, with its exciting buildings; the fish market in Hanover Street; the Muir Street bath house; the Mosque in Chapel Street; small houses in Reform Street; the intersection of Clifton and Vogelgezang Streets; an exciting house in Aspeling Street – although the ground floor was in ruins, part of the top floor remained intact.

I remember painting the Peninsula Maternity Home in Caledon Street. On the corner, past this stark building, was a shoe-maker working practically in the dark, with big rubbish bins outside, a large blue one and a badly dented brown one.

I painted a picture of the ruins of the wash-house – where in earlier times the washerwomen brought their 'madam's' washing. Glass was shattered in all the windows, the corrugated iron roof was battered and some of it had already been taken down. Inside, 'skollies' were taking whatever they could find.

In the late 1970s I also made a pen and ink sketch of the Salvation Army Barracks at the corner of Roger and Muir Street. Only the shell of the building was standing, with gaping holes where the windows had been. Lower down Muir Street, the Muir Street mosque was still intact, of course.

On the left, in Roger Street, there was a large empty field with the usual detritus of the bulldozers – broken bricks, rubble, odd shoes, old newspapers, tin cans, a dead rat, waste of every kind. The whole scene resembled a bomb site in London during the Blitz.

Sandra McGregor – 'Onse artist' in District Six

The National Cinema

Late 1970s
51 x 61cm
Pen, sepia ink and gouache
Signed bottom right

OWNER UNKNOWN

I loved the National Cinema and its fine Edwardian architecture. This was the last painting I did in District Six. The small shop inside the cinema on the left, that previously sold sweets and ice creams, had already closed. Two film posters are still up above the entrances, so perhaps they were waiting for a film to commence. There is despair in the painting: it depicts the silence which had blanketed District Six.

A dark blue lorry with yellow and red markings was parked there, and further on was a solitary house with people still living on the ground floor. The windows of the house were shattered, leaving black empty spaces, One of the windows was closed off with corrugated iron. There were about five steps leading up to the front door and the occupied side of the house, which I painted.

The colours merged from black to deep purple to alizarin crimson, and then on to cadmium red, light red and yellow. There was a yellow convertible parked in the street, in yellow ochre plus Naples yellow plus a touch of cadmium yellow. And there was a wash line extending the entire width of the field, with colourful washing blowing in the wind. In the background was St Mark's Church.

It was a wonderful scene – but very sad because, by this time, as far as buildings were concerned, District Six was dying. The Star had burnt down, the British and National had gone, the shebeen had gone and with it Big Sophie, with her happy smile and two long black pigtails. I was still painting, there were still children who ran to meet me with their welcoming cry, "Sandera, Sandera . . ."

◆

PART 3

The dustbins of District Six I shall never forget. Few stood straight up – the more interesting ones were badly dented, leaning far to the left or to the right. They were wonderful to paint – grey-blue, deep purple, light red, crimson, alizarin ... The smell of the dustbins of the District contributed to the endless smells of District Six like the tantalising smells of samoosas from the café in Caledon Street; the smell of coffee from the famous Crescent Restaurant in Hanover Street and, of course, the hot curries for which they were famous. This was the only restaurant I knew where coloureds and whites could meet together.

One of the greatest compliments paid to me was by a man who bought my works and said, "I buy your paintings because when I look at them, I smell District Six."

CHAPTER 15

Beyond the District

In 2007, we took Sandra to see what was once the centre of her life. Sandra looked on in amazement and utter sadness at the desolation. "Where is Hanover Street? Where is Caledon Street?" she cried.

While District Six was being destroyed, Sandra had to look for new subject matter. Her involvement with the church had deepened over the years and she discovered a new source of inspiration when she was commissioned in January 1969 to paint a portrait of Canon CT Wood, Archdeacon of Cape Town, for the St George's Cathedral Muniments Room. She worshipped at the cathedral each Sunday, and became well known to the clergy and congregation, and particularly friendly with the Dean of Cape Town, Ted King. She abhorred the apartheid regime and admired Dean King's resistance to government policy in those early turbulent years.

Detail of a 1969 photograph of Sandra painting Canon CT Wood, Senior Chaplain to the Anglican Archbishop of Cape Town, in his regalia as Primatial Cross Bearer to the Archbishop.

Sandra's palette is visible in the foreground as she adds finishing touches.

Sandra McGregor – 'Onse artist' in District Six

Portrait of Father Robert Mercer, Prior of the Community of the Resurrection
1969
91 x 71cm
Oil on board
No visible signature

PRIVATE COLLECTION

Father Robert Mercer posed for me in 1969. He wore the monk's habit of the Community of the Resurrection, with a thick black belt and a big button on the shoulder. He asked me to use a red background to show that he had turned his back on the world.

After the first commission, in the same year she painted a portrait of the Prior of the Community of the Resurrection at Stellenbosch, Father Robert Mercer. In 1970 she painted Father John da Costa of St Mark's Church, District Six, and in 1971 the Bishop Suffragan of Cape Town, the Right Reverend Philip Russell. During this time Father Ninian McManus, Roman Catholic chaplain at the University of Cape Town, also sat for her, but there is no record of this portrait.

FATHER ROBERT MERCER, Prior of the Community of the Resurrection at Stellenbosch, occasionally preached at the Cathedral in Cape Town, and after one such sermon Sandra asked him if he would pose for her.

Father Mercer held strong views on church matters, such as the ordination of women priests (which he could not accept), and the role of the church in the struggle against apartheid. He mixed freely with all races and was a friend of David Binns and Canon Wood. Sometimes he would invite Sandra to lunch with the other monks in Stellenbosch.

However, in September 1970 he and another Anglican priest in Stellenbosch were ordered to leave the country. The following short notice appeared in the press on the 25 September 1970:

> The Government has served deportation orders on two Anglican priests in Stellenbosch, the Rev. Robert Mercer and the Rev. Bernard Chamberlain, who must leave the country before the end of next month, according to the Nationalist Press.
>
> The reported move follows the distribution of a pamphlet recently among the Anglican congregation in Stellenbosch.
>
> The pamphlet discussed the decision of the World Council of Churches to give funds to terrorist organizations in Southern Africa.
>
> The Prime Minister, Mr. Vorster, later said in Parliament that he would be neglecting his duty if he did not take steps against the author of the pamphlet.
>
> Both are British, and have been in the country for two years.

Father Robert Mercer took his portrait with him to England when he left the country. He eventually moved to Canada, where he became a Bishop.

Bishop Philip Russell, Bishop Suffragan of Cape Town when Sandra painted his portrait in 1971, was later appointed Bishop of Port Elizabeth, and ultimately Archbishop of Cape Town. The whereabouts of this painting is unknown.

Sandra's illustration for St George's Cathedral Christmas card, 1970. Canon Cecil Wood discussed the project with her in her studio in Chapmill Court, and she chose to depict a small cathedral window by Gabriel Loire. Sandra used pen, ink and gouache on board, 106 x 45cm.

LEFT
Sandra sketching in the Cathedral, October 1969, against the immense backdrop of a stained-glass window.

IN ADDITION TO THE CLERGY PORTRAITS, Sandra was commissioned by Archbishop Selby-Taylor to design a Christmas card for St George's Cathedral to be sent out in December 1970. The Christmas card bore the following description of her work.

> Drawing by Sandra McGregor from a window by Gabriel Loire in St. George's Cathedral Cape Town. The right-hand light shows St. Anne standing behind the Virgin Mary who is holding the Christ Child, the left-hand light shows an outline of the Cape Peninsula with the star of navigation above, and across both the anchor of Good Hope. In the top tracery is the Archangel Gabriel, messenger of the Incarnation and patron saint of the artist.

In the early 1970s, Dean Ted King had selected the French artist Gabriel Loire to execute window panels for St. George's Cathedral, Cape Town. He produced beautiful stained-glass windows which now adorn the Nave, the North and South transepts and the Gallery. He also designed The Great West Window which celebrates South Africa's newly-won freedom and is a symbol of national liberation and reconciliation. It is a permanent memorial to one of the world's most optimistic liberation stories. The panel was dedicated in 1983 by Philip Russell His Grace the Archbishop of Cape Town, and the Dedication was led by Dean Ted King.

St George's Cathedral assumed an increasingly high profile as a centre of political protest and resistance under Archbishop Desmond Tutu.

Sketch of squatters,
St George's Cathedral
1982
40 x 50cm
Cray-pas on strawboard
No visible signature

ST GEORGE'S CATHEDRAL

The room in the cathedral was dark, lit only by a single lamp which gave a wonderful effect of chiaroscuro, dramatic and mysterious. I did a quick sketch with cray-pas on strawboard intending to come back the next day to complete it. However, during the night the squatters slipped away without a word to anyone. This preliminary sketch still hangs in the cathedral.

Protesting students – dragged, kicked and punched by police on the cathedral steps in 1972 – were received by Dean King with open arms as he flung open the cathedral doors. Many people were touched by his compassion, leadership and friendship. Sandra was close to Ted King in these turbulent years and admired him greatly.

In 1982 over fifty squatters, evicted from their illegal dwellings, sought protection from the police and sanctuary in the cathedral. These men stayed in the cathedral for a few days – with Dean Ted King arranging food for them. The congregation was asked to help and Sandra, aware of what was happening, approached Ted King for permission to draw the squatters.

179

Sandra McGregor – 'Onse artist' in District Six

Portrait of the Bishop Suffragan of Cape Town, the Right Reverend Philip Russell.
1971
91 x 71cm
Oil on canvas
No visible signature

PRIVATE COLLECTION

This three-quarter length portrait in oil, focuses on his hands. On retirement, Bishop Russell followed his family and emigrated to Australia.

SANDRA'S SKILL as a portrait painter brought her other private commissions. Dr Reeve Sanders, the Medical Superintendent of Groote Schuur Hospital knew Sandra's father, and they had met several times. Occasionally Sandra was invited to supper with Dr Sanders and her husband in their house on the rocks near Sea Point.

Other portrait commissions came from Carmella Seeff, wife of Geoffrey Seeff, a well-known property developer and businessman, and two of Carmella's friends, Dr Peter Maytham a leading Cape Town ear, nose and throat specialist, and his daughter, Wendy Maytham.

WHEN SANDRA PAINTED the portrait of Father Ninian Macmanus in 1970/71, he suggested she approach the Cape Technical College for Advanced Education for a teaching post. Mr Fourie, the Head of the Art Department, knew her work and immediately invited her to join the staff. Sandra taught drawing and painting to evening classes of adults, while producing her own work during the day. It was another way of supplementing her income. When the college closed in 1976, Mr Fourie gave Sandra four wooden 'donkeys' (easels), which had been used by the art students. They came in useful when Sandra put them in her flat at Chapmill Court, where she proceeded to give private classes. Two students in particular, Johann Strydom and Malinda du Randt, became close friends.

Malinda saw a small advertisement in *The Argus*. 'Private tuition, three-dimensional drawing, Sandra McGregor'. "I wanted to learn and she taught me everything I know. She saw that I had talent and she developed it. She started by making me draw a ball of wool on a table… She was an amazing teacher and I will be forever grateful to her."

Johann Strydom praised Sandra too. "Sandra gave us a list of colours – compulsory ones and additional ones – and lecture notes. She was very strict and only allowed these specific colours: she forbade anyone to have burnt umber in their boxes."

BESIDES TEACHING and painting portraits, Sandra's urge to paint and her endless energy led her to record Cape Town city scenes: interesting buildings and threatened landmarks. In January 1968, she painted a scene in Wale Street, near St George's Cathedral, one of Cape Town's most historic streets. Onlookers watched Sandra paint and the Argus of 11 January published a picture of her at work.

Sandra viewed the scene from the steps of St George's Cathedral,

Portrait of Dr Reeve Sanders
Early 1970s
57 x 52cm
Pen, sepia ink and gouache
Signed bottom right

Dr Sanders had a strong personality and insisted on being painted in her working clothes, with the watch which she always wore around her neck.

PRIVATE COLLECTION

Portrait of Carmella Seeff

Early 1970s
57 x 52cm
Pen, sepia ink and gouache
No visible signature

PRIVATE COLLECTION

Carmella asked me to go with her to buy a suitable dress for the sitting. We chose one with feathers around the neck and, during the sittings as Carmella breathed, the feathers moved slightly. Carmella's long earrings came from a trip to Israel, soon after the Six-Day War in 1967.

Portrait of Dr Maytham
early 1970s
57 x 52cm
Oil on board
Signed bottom right

PRIVATE COLLECTION

Dr Maytham looked after me, pro bono, for many years. When his sight started to fail he could no longer perform fine surgical work. He transferred to Groote Schuur to run the physiotherapy department where he assessed patients. Sadly, in his later years he lost his sight completely.

Portrait of Wendy Maytham
early 1970s
57 x 52cm
Pen, sepia ink and gouache on paper
Signed bottom right

PRIVATE COLLECTION

Wendy Maytham's father chose the dress for her portrait. Tragically, soon after both portraits were completed, when riding on the beach Wendy's horse slipped, threw her, and she died – aged nineteen or twenty.

Portrait of Daniela Capocecera,
early 1970s
57 x 52cm
Pen, sepia ink and gouache on paper
Signed bottom right

PRIVATE COLLECTION

An Italian family from Rome lived in Chapmill Court. Their daughter, Daniela, in her twenties, sat for me in the 1970s.

Beyond the District

Teaching came naturally to Sandra and she held classes in her flat at Chapmill Court. The children are Catherine, daughter of Daphne Hill, a Roedean classmate of Sandra's, and Barry Whitmill. These private classes continued for many years.

opposite the Board of Executors building, with a Florentine lamp on the corner. Prominent companies and legal practices had offices in this building. Across St. George's Street was Newspaper House, the offices of the Cape Times. Another building bears the sign GENERAL ESTATE* ORPHAN CHAMBER. This building, designed by Thomas Inglesby one of the first Cape Town architects, was erected in 1865.

A PAINTING of the South African Library was commissioned by Frank Bradlow, eminent Cape Town art collector and philanthropist. The origins of the Library date back to 1818 when Lord Charles Somerset, Governor of the Cape Colony, founded the South African Public Library. A neoclassical building, based on the Fitzwilliam Museum in Cambridge, England, the South African Public Library was opened in 1860.

Many collections were made over the years, one of the most notable being that of Sir George Grey in 1861 who presented the Library with his personal collection of medieval and Renaissance manuscripts and rare books. Renamed the South African Library in 1967, Sandra painted it in April 1968. The painting hung there for many years.

IN 1664 THERE HAD BEEN RUMOURS of war between Britain and the Netherlands and an attack by the British upon the Dutch East India Company's small replenishment station at the Cape of Good Hope was feared. This Company – the Vereenigde Oost-Indische Compagnie, known

Sandra McGregor – 'Onse artist' in District Six

The South African Library

1968
41 x 51cm
Pen, ink and gouache
No visible signature

PRIVATE COLLECTION

I decided to paint this remarkable building from above and persuaded Dean King of St George's Cathedral, to provide a 'reference letter' to the Supreme Court vouching for my trustworthiness and ability. On the strength of this endorsement, I was allowed to paint from the rooftop of the Supreme Court building in Queen Victoria Street.

To get there, I was taken through many numbers of doors and up even more flights of stairs to a large room in which hundreds of valuable books were stored. Another flight of stairs led to a trapdoor which opened onto the roof. I carried my basket of paints and brushes, but others helped carry my table and chairs – all of which were taken down at the end of each day, to be repeated and re-assembled the following morning.

The Kat Balcony

1971
47 x 59 cm
Pen, sepia ink and gouache
Signed bottom right

THE SAUNDERS COLLECTION
TONGAAT HULETT GROUP
KWAZULU-NATAL

Reproduced from a photographic print

I loved working within the historic walls of the Castle, and recorded the balcony in intricate detail, with the stairs leading up to the majestic double doors and the exquisite Italian lamps The archway and large sundial on the wall can be clearly seen, and I was shown how to read the time.

Lady Anne Barnard, wife of the Colonial Secretary at the Cape of Good Hope and official hostess of the then British Governor, lived at the Cape from 1797 to 1802. She would have entered the castle through these balcony doors many times. Her journals depicting life at the Cape under British occupation, were later published to much acclaim.

as the VOC – began work on the first permanent European fortification in the Cape, and by 1669 a pentagonal castle built out of stone was completed. Inside the Castle were living quarters, shops, a bakery, a church, workshops and cells. The Kat Balcony was built in 1695. All judicial sentences were read from this balcony, official visitors were welcomed to the Castle, and announcements were made to soldiers, slaves and burghers of the Cape. The balcony was redesigned by Louis Michel Thibault and rebuilt between 1786 and 1790.

Sandra was commissioned to paint this balcony, and a large picture of her at work appeared in the press on 28 July 1971.

> Artist Sandra McGregor has become a familiar figure to soldiers in the courtyard of the Castle, Cape Town. She is painting many of the historic features of the Castle and is seen here with her version of the historic 'Kat Balcony', incorporating the famous archway and sundial. Watching her at work is Major C.R. Clarke.

ANOTHER LANDMARK in Cape Town was the Alhambra Theatre in Riebeeck Street. Designed in 1928 by the architect P Rogers Cooke, the theatre opened in 1929 as a cinema house with sufficient stage facilities for theatrical shows or operas. The exterior design, with its almost 'Moorish' facade was different from anything in Cape Town at the time.

Sandra had a deep affinity for architecture and, in particular, for any distinctive building about to be demolished. She sought permission to sit on the rooftop balcony of the old South African Broadcasting Corporation building across the road from the Alhambra, in order to paint the intricate exterior. It took her about four weeks to complete the painting.

This unique building, which had lured so many people through its doors over the years, and given them such pleasure, was demolished to make way for a modern, rectangular office block, Shell House. To Sandra's knowledge there is no other painting of the Alhambra.

A concerned article appeared in the Argus newspaper on the 21 January 1972.

> **ALHAMBRA ON CANVAS**
>
> When the old Alhambra goes and, tomorrow night its curtain will come down for the last time, it will leave a gap in 'old' Cape Town like a missing front tooth in a well-loved face.
>
> For those of us who dimly remember its opening night half a lifetime ago – how we children marvelled at the 'stars' and the

The Alhambra Theatre

1972
55 x 77cm
Pen, sepia ink and gouache
Signed bottom left

SHELL SA ENERGY

The atmospheric interior featured a dark blue sky, twinkling stars and cloud effects on the high, vaulted ceiling, the Alhambra *operated as one of Cape Town's major cinemas for many years and was renowned for its décor. Numerous stage shows were presented well into the 1960s, as well as operas such as* Rigoletto *and* La Traviata, *performed by touring companies of mainly Italian singers. A Wurlitzer pipe organ had originally been installed, but was moved to the* Bijou Theatre *in Salt River in 1931, and finally to the* Nico Malan *(now the* Artscape) Theatre, Cape Town, *in 1998.*

cloud effect on the high, vaulted ceiling! – the nostalgia at the thought of that last curtain is acute.

It was a little consoling, therefore, to learn that the Cape Town artist, Sandra McGregor, is painting the well-loved face of the Alhambra. At least there will be this record for posterity.

Many facets

Petite Sandra … is a girl with a feeling for old things, for yesterday's beauty. Her artist's eye is quick to pick up the old city's architectural charms – so often missed by the less observant or the uncaring.

She saw the beauty of the shabbiness of District Six as it used to be, and captured its many facets on dozens of canvases. More recently she has been painting inside Cape Town's Castle (the insignificant, original lamps on the Slave Balcony were one of many subjects), and the historic Roeland Street jail.

Now, across the road from the Alhambra, on a balcony looking down on its familiar face, she is sketching in the preliminary outlines of her painting.

Exhibition

We are lucky to have our Sandra McGregors. The Victorian face of 'old' Cape Town is changing so quickly that even the oldest of us already have difficulty remembering what it looked like only 20 years ago.

One of these days Sandra will be having a full-scale exhibition of her works in Cape Town, and that will be something worth waiting for – a mirror reflecting the city's past…

IN 1971 Sandra selected another unusual building, Roeland Street Prison, which as far as Sandra has been able to establish, no other artist ever painted. 'Doc' de Villiers, Sandra's Stellenbosch friend, had suggested this subject to her knowing that the prison would ultimately be used to house the State Archives.

On the first afternoon Sandra positioned herself on the pavement across the road to make some sketches. To her astonishment four plain-clothes policemen stopped their cars and demanded to see the letter giving her permission to draw and paint the prison. They also confiscated her sketches. At the time, photographing or drawing prisons was prohibited. Realising she would get nowhere without permission, she went to Caledon

Wale Street

Early 1970s
41 x 51cm
Pen, sepia ink and gouache
Signature bottom right, trimmed

OWNER UNKNOWN

The woman in the blue uniform in the forefront is Susan, a cleaner from the cathedral whom I knew. Susan saw me painting and asked if I would put her in the picture. I agreed and told her to go and stand next to the street pole. Children were always in the streets, and there are three looking quizzically at me.

Square Police Station, where she saw Colonel Jan Grobbelaar, who was most courteous and helpful. She explained her reason for wanting to paint the prison, and was given a typed form granting her permission 'om die Gevangenis te skets'.

Sandra had already decided to include the blue police van that arrived every day with prisoners. She had to go to a different police department for permission to paint the van. She was warned not to paint any prisoners in the van: the penalty for doing so would be R200 or two years in prison.

Armed with her letter, she rang the bell of the prison. A small square peephole slid open to reveal a beady eye. Sandra said that she had permission to paint the prison and held up her letter. After a while she heard the sound of keys, the door opened and she was told to enter.

It was dark inside, so dark that there was an electric light burning. The warder instructed her to follow him.

> *I scanned the scene: some prisoners sat at a large table, and others were standing nearby. I smiled and said, "Good morning", and each man put his hand over his eyes and turned his face away. Meneer Prins and Meneer Smit, the two head warders, explained that these white men were ashamed of being seen in gaol by a woman. I was to discover, to my amusement, that coloured prisoners had a totally different attitude.*

Meneer Prins asked her how she was going to set about painting. Sandra explained that she would need two chairs and a table, if possible, for her art equipment – pencils, pen and ink, palette, gouache paints and brushes, water jar, blotting paper and a cloth. Most of the equipment was in a shopping bag on wheels, but her many brushes and palette she carried herself in a basket. Meneer Prins said that Sandra could use the large table that she had seen when first entering the prison. Then, to her surprise he instructed two coloured prisoners to carry all her 'equipment', including the large table and two chairs. The two prisoners, staggering under the weight, beside them a warder armed with a gun, hefted this load into the street.

> *I have often smiled to myself at what the busy traffic officers and car drivers must have thought, forced to wait for us to cross the busy road to get to the pavement on the other side. This went on for six weeks, every day except Sunday.*

SANDRA HAD A CLEAR VIEW of the prison from where she sat. Many people came to stand around and watch her at work. One man, a white man, said,

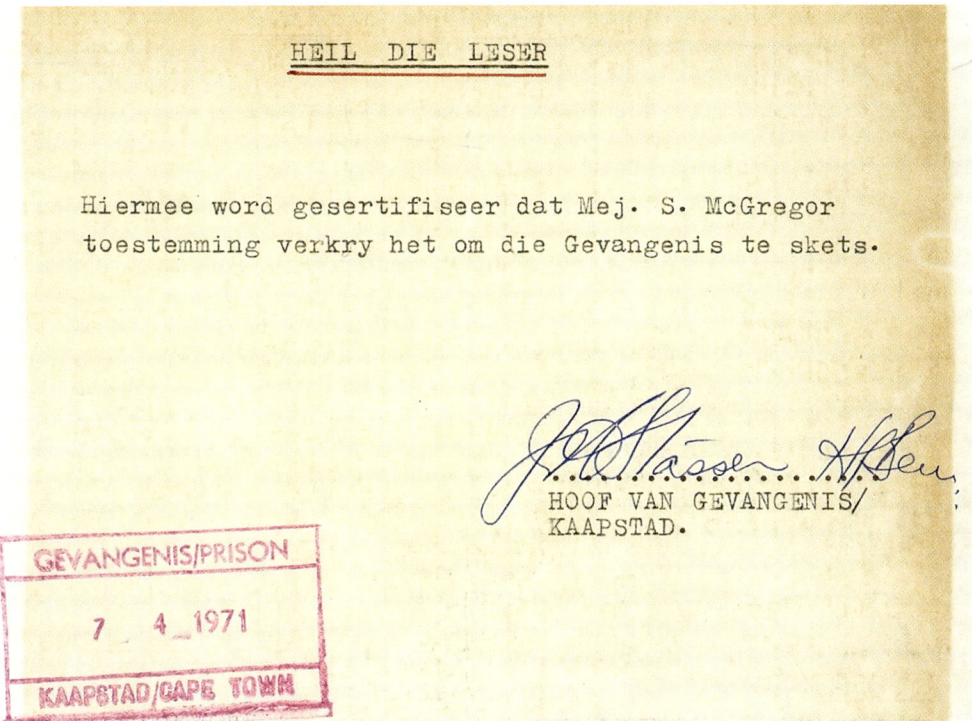

Sandra's letter of permission to paint the Roeland Street Prison.

"I don't know how you can bear to paint that prison – there are men suffering in there you know." The head warder had said that at four o'clock each day, a policeman would stand just outside the prison and wave a white handkerchief to signal it was time for her to stop painting and leave. Every day, the two prisoners and the armed warder would cross the road, help pack up her equipment, and return to the prison.

Each morning, a warder opened the door for her, she entered the room with the single light bulb burning, with the white prisoners waiting. She was refused permission to paint the prison a second time because of the white prisoners and their shame and embarrassment.

Her coloured friends felt otherwise. Each afternoon, between four and four-thirty, a lorry stopped in front of the prison and an armed coloured warder would jump down from the lorry, followed by a large number of coloured prisoners. That first afternoon the prisoners jumped out and looking around they saw her. Immediately they waved and shouted excitedly, "Miss artist! Miss artist!" Prison to these men did not carry the stigma of shame: besides, many of them knew Roeland Street well.

Meneer Smit and Meneer Prins had been in the prison service a long time, and were always cooperative and helpful. I believe it was because I had met and painted many former prisoners, and was interested in their lives in prison. Near completion, I added to the painting, in the manner in which children draw, the driver of the

Sandra McGregor – 'Onse artist' in District Six

Roeland Street Prison

1971
41 x 51cm
Pen, sepia ink and gouache
No visible signature

OWNER UNKNOWN

During the 1970s the prison housed a staff of 80 and approximately 850 prisoners. It could not be modernised economically to comply with the requirements of the Department of Prisons and in 1975 It was announced that the prison was to be closed. In April 1977 the last 214 awaiting-trial prisoners were transferred to Pollsmoor Prison. In November 1989 the National Archives and Records Service took possession of the building, specifically modified to house the Cape Town Archives.

blue van and a couple of policemen. The police were not pleased but allowed me to leave these egg-figures as I had painted them.

The day after the painting was finished Sandra took it to show Julian Adler, in his shop in town. On seeing it, one of his customers in the shop immediately wanted to buy it. It was sold to a Miss Botha for R200, paid off monthly, and its whereabouts is now unknown. The price was more than Sandra had received for any earlier work of District Six.

I forgot the advice of my friend, 'Doc' de Villiers, in Stellenbosch.
"Do not sell the painting but keep it, and sell it when Roeland Street Prison becomes the State Archives."
Needing cash as always, I could not wait.

SANDRA'S FIRST EXHIBITION was held at the Regency Art Gallery in 1963, the second at St George's Cathedral in 1967, and another at the Anglican Church, Stellenbosch, in the mid-1970s. In 1978, a major exhibition of her work was held at Stuttafords Gallery, Cavendish Square. Bruce Heilbuth wrote about this in an article, entitled DISTRICT SIX, published on 19 April 1978, together with an appealing photograph of Sandra at fifty.

SANDRA McGREGOR ... will hold a major exhibition of her work at Stuttafords Gallery, Cavendish Square, from Friday.

The biggest items on display will be 22 oil panels. Their subject matter will be personalities and places in District 6.

Her artistic record of the once notorious 'district', in the days when it was still a thriving centre of commerce, domesticity – and crime – is one of the most comprehensive on canvas…

…although many of her paintings have been sold and dispersed, a good cross-section will be shown in the Cavendish exhibition.

In addition to the large oil panels there will be no fewer than 190 other paintings.

They include many samples of Miss McGregor's 'fantasy phase', a new and imaginative trend in her work. They were influenced by her study of the philosophy of Karl Jung and take many forms and themes – including religion.

One of the most unusual aspects of her exhibition … will be a miniature theatre, operated by the talented puppeteer, Mrs Ray Querido.

Again, the accent will be on District 6 characters, which Sandra McGregor has painted in miniature.

They include hadjis, washerwomen, fruit barrow-boys, the former Rector of St Mark's in District 6, John da Costa (now Dean of Salisbury), and many other indigenous types.

Their appearance on the tiny stage will be accompanied by appropriate music recorded by Mrs Querido.

The miniature puppet theatre and all 56 little figures (see Sandra's people of District Six (Page 205), painted by Sandra in gouache, have been recently located and photographed. They form part of the District Six Museum's collection.

The Little Theatre was made by Ray Querido and her husband. Each of Sandra's 56 figures was fixed to a spatula so that they could be moved around the stage. Ray wrote the story of District Six and the play was full of love, music, dancing and happiness … then, one by one the figures 'died' and the buildings came down.

ALL THE 'FANTASY' PAINTINGS produced in Ray Querido's flat have gone, some to St Luke's Hospice where they were sold, others given away. The remaining few were sold at Sandra's fourth and final exhibition in 1990. There are no photographs or records of any of these.

This exhibition, entitled 'My District Six', was held at the Baxter Gallery of Art, 21 November – 15 December 1990. There were 41 paintings on show. In addition, there were 20 'fantasies'. Prices ranged from R50 to R2,000, with nine priced in four figures. Twelve were not for sale. It is interesting to note that *The Cross* was exhibited, on loan from St Cyprian's Church in Retreat.

The exhibition was sponsored by The Board of Executors and opened by the Very Reverend Colin Jones, Dean of St George's Cathedral, who commented on the contradictory nature of the people of District Six and related this to life.

> (These works) speak at one and the same time, of a vibrant, exotic unique community called 'District Six' and of a slum – with all the pain and trauma that poverty brings … All these paintings are about life – real and imaginary. The faces and places which made up this District played their magic on Sandra McGregor and she was moved to put life on strawboard, masonite and canvas…
>
> … Sandra McGregor has captured some of these people in her work, immortalising them in sometimes rough but always loving paintwork… [she] won the hearts of the people she painted and was given the joyous and frightening privilege of being taken into this place which became known as the heart of Cape Town…
>
> … By giving us a look at her paintings, her experiences, Sandra McGregor is helping to keep hope alive – the Hope that one day soon one contradiction will be laid to rest – that a city without its people is no city. As a child of District Six it is my honour and privilege to declare open this exhibition of District Six reflections – a personal gift of an artist who lost her heart but not her hope that one day soon there will once again be children who will speak of 'My District Six'.

Opposition to the erection of new buildings in District Six became so intense that by 1988 only a few buildings had been constructed. Vacant land where the District housed its inhabitants stands as a poignant unofficial memorial.

IN THE 1990s Sandra's health deteriorated and she could no longer live alone. She moved to the Ladies Christian Home, Gardens, on 11 October, 1994 where she still lives. It is a big room and accommodates her table, easel and art equipment, with a large, high bay window giving good light. She still does pencil portraits on commission, and sometimes just draws for pleasure. At 81 she has not lost her touch.

◆

EPILOGUE

A remarkable heritage

Sandra McGregor at her desk in the Ladies Christian Home, Cape Town. She is clutching her precious 'skollie' belt.

Sandra's life, which started out with such promise and so many privileges, descended through turbulent times to solitary old age and – in many people's minds – no success in her work. With hindsight, she has been successful. Her legacy is a valuable and unique record of an era of life in District Six.

She had courage, endurance and the resilience to survive; she created art with care, respect and accuracy; she saw something beautiful in the mysteriousness of District Six. She still feels wonder and excitement in describing the 'inside' of the District, not just the 'outside'. She portrayed the look, the smell, the taste, the feel of the District. Her art expressed her passionate feelings. Hard-working and skilful, she had the vision and ability to capture the moment, speaking directly to us, preserving the legend of District Six as she saw it. It is a remarkable heritage for South Africa.

The future her father envisaged for her, that of a great portrait painter in London, is fulfilled instead by the unique paintings she produced as a solitary woman painting in the heart of District Six. Her frequent presence, childlike trust, warm interest in everyone, and her dedicated recording on canvas of the District and its people, in a seemingly dangerous and shunned world, is worth more than her father could ever have imagined.

Sandra sacrificed much for her chosen vocation: she never married, never owned a home of her own, nor a car; had no children and no family close by. She could not afford to travel again, and was always impecunious.

In her life, she experienced love, passion, joy, jealousy, illness, and loneliness, yet her work was her strength. She remains remarkably cheerful and has devoted friends. Those who gathered at my house in 1995 to meet Sandra after many years are still in close touch with her.

May this book, written for Sandra, serve as testimony to friendship and as a memorial to *her* District Six. May Sandra's art receive the praise and acknowledged place it deserves in the history of Cape Town and in South African art.

Dolores Fleischer
Cape Town
February 2010

AFTERWORD

Now, today, I can say that the heartbeat of Cape Town, the fun, the laughter, the joy, the sadness, the pain, died with District Six. Gone are the street corners where the corner-boys used to stand. Gone is the Church Lads Brigade marching up Caledon Street, with bugles blowing and flags flying. Gone is the sound of the Snoek Cart – that unforgettable sound which was used by the SA Radio piece, 'Snoek Town Calling'. Gone are the crowds in Caledon Street and Hanover Street on Saturday mornings, doing their weekly shopping.

I remember especially the beautiful Indian women in their saris and magnificent jewellery, I remember my friends the 'bergies', especially Jan who lived on cane spirit and whose skin was a strange colour pink. Once, when I sat painting in Hanover Street, Jan came reeling along, full of spirits, mutilating himself with a razor blade. I remember Caledon Street after dark, for I had been working late, the glow of candles and lamplight in the windows; it was now winter and very cold, and I saw some of my 'skollies' standing on a field around a brazier for warmth. They invited me to join them, which I did, and never shall I forget the firelight which played on their faces, turning them into living Rembrandt portraits. Nobody can take from me my memories of my District Six, twenty incredible and marvellous years.

I have written that the heartbeat of Cape Town died with District Six. But District Six did not die. She lives on in the hearts of all her people. The buildings died, the bioscopes were demolished and became bricks and mortar. The homes were bulldozed down.

But recently I walked over a field near the Oriental Plaza. There were weeds and bricks and rubbish, but stand very still, as I did, and the wind will bring you the voices of District Six, talking, laughing, singing. And all around me came the spirits of District Six, the children of District Six running to meet me as they always did, "Sandera ... Sandera ..." And then, one by one came all the men, women and children that I had drawn and painted, luminous shapes, dancing in the wind.

So you see, the SPIRIT of District Six lives on, in the hearts of all that loved her – and that can never die.

Sandra McGregor
Cape Town

ACKNOWLEDGEMENTS

FINDING SANDRA has been a journey of immense interest, purpose, excitement and satisfaction. Thank you Sandra for taking me into your life and sharing it with me. You agreed that I should write your story, and enthusiastically committed yourself to this project. You gave me notes and hours of conversation, and together we located many of your paintings and met many of your District Six friends. It may be unique that the author and artist of a book such as this were childhood friends, and that after many decades that friendship continues. It has been a privilege for me to write about you, Sandra. Thank you.

So many other people have helped and encouraged me, and to them I give my most grateful thanks –

- **Barbara Long-Innes** walked every step of the way with me, commenting, discussing and editing the text, making wise suggestions and sharing with me her deep and compassionate knowledge of Sandra. Her constant enthusiasm gave me courage.
- **Professor Tom Bothwell** read an early version of the text, commenting with meticulous care and professional thoroughness.
- **Patty Kolbe** edited a later version, and with her husband **Vincent Kolbe** made sure certain statements pertaining to District Six and its people were correct. Their fundamental knowledge of that era and place was inspiring, their enthusiasm uplifting. Patty's comments and suggestions were invaluable.
- **Julian Adler** was a staunch supporter of the whole project and old friend of Sandra's. His knowledge of her, her artwork and the time in which she was painting in District Six proved an invaluable source of fact and confirmation. He also located many of her paintings for me.
- **Sandy Prosalendis**, with her unfailing faith in the importance of the book spurred me on, and gave her cheerful help so positively. Her introduction of the Kolbes to this project was a bonus.
- **Mrs Elizabeth Raby**, general manager of the Ladies Christian Home, courteously and kindly made it possible to photograph Sandra's paintings in a convenient and suitable room.
- **Michael Hall** was the willing, cooperative and highly skilled photographer of most of the images for this book. His professionalism and attention to detail was remarkable, as was his kindness to Sandra whenever they met.
- **Ruphen Courdyzer**, professional photographer in Johannesburg, worked with skill for the project, tracking down and photographing the paintings I had located there. **Jeffery Cross** and **Eyal Gordon** were professional photographers of paintings held in America.
- **Zena Potash** and **Cindy Yeoman** in California so promptly and willingly sent images of the paintings in their possession. Zena's kindness to Sandra on a recent visit to Cape Town was also memorable.

- **Rochelle Keene**, curator of the Adler Museum of Medicine, Johannesburg, sent me important documents regarding Sandra's father, Lee McGregor.
- **Francois Roux**, artist and old friend of Sandra, gave time to look at an album of Sandra's collected work and encouraged me by pronouncing her, "a very fine artist".
- **Father Anthony Langenhoven** had the large cross in St Cyprian's Church in Retreat taken down for photographing and welcomed us warmly to his precinct.
- **All the collectors** who were approached, willingly made it possible for McGregor paintings to be photographed in their homes, and **various organisations** which held Sandra's work cooperated warmly and fully.
- **The descendants** of Sandra's District Six friends gave me so much information about 'Onse artist': Aziza Cassiem and her family, Cass Gordon, Vinod Vasson, Nazima Ahrense and her family; and Fareed Rossier.
- **Old friends** Shirley Arnold, Gillian Meyer, Jenny Mason, her brother Richard Mason, and the SAORA (South African Old Roedeanian Association), all showed great friendship for and interest in Sandra, and enthusiasm for this project. Their constant support has been remarkable.

I have been most fortunate in working with Robin Stuart-Clark, publisher, who immediately saw the potential of this project and its importance, and who, with his team, produced this outstanding book. I thank him most sincerely for his support, encouragement, advice, friendship and professional skill, which I shall always remember.

My sons, Lance and Kevin Fleischer, never failed in their interest and appreciation of my work. Lance read the text and commented; Kevin gave good advice and support; his belief and encouragement in this project never wavered.

Without the encouragement and support of my dear, caring husband, Anthony Fleischer, who also believed deeply in this project, was excited about it and did not mind my commitment to long hours of work, I would never have persevered. As always, he was a perfect companion and sounding board all the way.

Finally, my greatest debt is to Spencer Fleischer, my eldest son, who realised that this story should be written. His persistent encouragement and deep determination to see this book in print pushed me on when I faltered. His reading of various drafts of the text, his ideas and suggestions, his AppleMac production of an album of Sandra's paintings, kept the development of the project on track. With foresight he estimated from the start what a valuable contribution it would make to the social and art history of the Cape. The project is completed, and I think he was right. I cannot thank him enough for all he did.

Dolores Fleischer
Cape Town
February 2010

Appendix 1 – Sandra's notes on the basic methods of the old masters

As taught by Helmut Ruhemann, Head Restorer of the National Gallery, London.

Paint with turpentine only. Never use linseed oil. For strong, individual brushwork use bristle brushes. Use semi-absorbent grounds.

Starting a picture

Begin by drawing-in using pencil or charcoal. Fix with fixative. Then go over this drawing with blue oil paint; model with the paint. But don't lay in dark shadows. Shadows must always be thin and transparent. Lights thin and opaque.

Paint vividly and spontaneously, modelling with your brush.

Remember that lights will not tell on white, so the darker and stronger the half-tone beneath them, the more they will vibrate.

Beauty of colour lies not in its strength, but in its clarity and precision. Go for precision and variegation ie, changing from one colour to another, which makes it interesting and rich.

The great secret lies in the half-tones.

To achieve the real Titian effect and to make your highlights tell, lay in a general yellow tone, raw sienna for example (over your fixed pencil or charcoal drawing). You can use Tempera dried powder pigment, because it dries so quickly. Best purchased in London at Winsor and Newton.

The Old Masters painted over a yellow ground, for example, using tempera paint to get the understatement, as termed by Eric Newton; use no strong light and no strong dark. You are 'groping', finding your way. Use flake white for the understatement and zinc white for the alla prima. It is rarely necessary to use Titanium white. The understatement can also be laid in with oil paint and turps.

El Greco, Goya and Rembrandt used dark brown, dark red and grey-toned grounds for speed. Rembrandt builds impasto over very dark colour.

If you lose the half tones, you will stop the form going round. (This is the basis of Monumental drawing and painting).

Tintoretto's deep carmine reds were underpainted in green-grey, and transparent carmine or alizarin was glazed on top. Only here or there did he allow patches of brilliant carmine.

Leonardo underpainted blue with green – a dim olive green. A touch of Prussian blue to yellow ochre gives a good green for underpainting. A blue sky was underpainted with a very light green blue, then pure ultramarine was glazed on top.

Rembrandt is the greatest of all the Masters for me – but I will not even attempt to describe his marvellous techniques of painting.

I will end, however, by saying what a joy and privilege it was to study with Helmut Ruhemann and to go round the National Gallery with him, whilst he opened my eyes to the techniques of the greatest painters of all time. He shared my love of Rembrandt, and used to say that no artist can paint more than he is himself, that the spirituality of Rembrandt flowed from his heart and soul into his work.

Stand in front of one of his masterpieces and LISTEN to what it says to you.

Sandra's palette

Davy's grey	Prussian blue
Naples yellow	Cobalt blue
Yellow ochre	Cobalt green
Raw sienna	Terra verte
Cadmium lemon	Viridian
Cadmium orange	Zinc or flake white
Cadmium red light	Cobalt violet light and dark
Cadmium red dark	{ warm ground tone / cool half tone
Alizarin crimson	
Light red	{ warm shadow / cool highlight
Cerulean blue	
Ultramarine	

Appendix 2 – Sandra's people of District Six

AMAAR – Member of the DKs. Handsome, well-built, wore tight jeans, bright shirts, a gold earring in one ear. He posed for me several times. He died of a heart attack.

ARTHUR – I met him practising for the 'Coon Carnival'. He sang well. Arthur made me my 'skollie' belt. Sitting at the top of Caledon Street he knocked 121 studs through the hard black leather. I used to wear it every day and still treasure it.

BERNIE – He was in the same gang, the Stalag 17s, as Ernie and Gillie, and often involved in gang fights. I dressed a thigh wound for him once, and he was always grateful for this.

BOB – The doorman of the National Cinema. He is in my painting of the *National Cinema at night* (Page 156).

BOETE LEIMAN – Boete owned a greengrocer's shop, which he ran with his brother – *Boete Leiman's Fruit and Vegetable Shop* (Page 168).

BONES – He was small and very thin, hence his nickname. He also features in the *National Cinema at night*, (Page 156) standing in the box office, wearing a balaclava cap. He was later stabbed to death in a gang fight.

BOSS – Lived in the 'Big House' at the Seven Steps, notorious for its comings and goings. Its blue door was always kept securely locked. He spent a lot of time watching the street from an upstairs window.

BROERTJIE – Gangleader. I visited him in Pollsmoor.

The figures illustrated here represent a selection of the cast produced by Sandra for her District Six Theatre.

BUCK JONES (BASIL JONES) – I met Buck in 1962, soon after my arrival in Cape Town. He worked for an Afrikaans magazine, *Ster*, and later became a sculptor. He introduced me to District Six and became my guardian and inspiration.

CASS GORDON (also known as **BERNIE**) – He was one of the first people I met in District Six. He had a hairdressing salon, 'Maison Cass' in Hanover Street and was a talented dancer. He owned a pink convertible and often drove me around in the District. I painted several portraits of Cass.

CHARLIE – A hairdresser and dancer who posed for his portrait in his dragon shirt. Charlie gave me several new shirts when he saw I needed them.

CHILDREN – Arthur (my favourite), Ronnie, Toyer, Henry, Alfie, Armien. They frequently gathered around when I was painting out of doors.

CLAUDE – A hawker who sold fruit and vegetables from his barrow.

COLONEL JAN GROBBELAAR – Head of Security Police at Caledon Square, who became very interested in my work. and often came to my flat in Chapmill Court to see my paintings. He would talk about police work and District Six. He was always kind and courteous.

DAVID POTASH – Father of Zena Potash, grew up in poverty in District Six and became a well-known jeweller in Cape Town. His wife **MIRIAM** died some years ago. **ZENA**, their daughter, is a psychiatrist who lives and practises in California.

DKs – The Dynamite Kids, a well-known gang, mostly in their twenties.

DEAN OF CAPE TOWN, THE VERY REVEREND EL KING – A revered figure in church circles, he was Dean for thirty years. He allowed me to bring some 'skollies' to the Cathedral when I held an exhibition there.

DOOS – Friend of Bernie, Ernie and Gillie, but older. He always wore a grey hat and posed for me. I went to his trial after he was arrested.

DUKE – A sailor, later a carpenter, a powerful man with dark piercing eyes. He posed for two portraits. He was married and lived in a room next to Banks Hiring Supply in Hanover Street.

ERNIE – I visited him in Groote Schuur after Gillie had stabbed him in the face. Shorter than the others, he had fair hair and blue eyes, and his son was the image of him.

FAREED ROSSIER – As a little boy he watched me painting in District Six. He is now a well-known practising artist in Cape Town.

FATHER JOHN DA COSTA – Priest at St Mark's Church, Cape Town. Born in the East End of London, he was a courageous man, well used to breaking up fighting in the streets.

GELAGGIES – He was well-known in District Six and walked with a limp. He usually carried a sack over his back. I never knew what was in it. I included him in my painting of Mr Lewis' shop (Page 142).

GILLIE – Tall and thin, he sold drugs. He was often caught and sent to prison and was soon out, selling again. He stabbed his friend Ernie in Motjie Ragmat's backyard.

GLOBE GANG – Ou Vyf had been head of this famous gang in the 1920s.

HANNES, THE FISHERMAN – A big, hefty man, he 'looked' like a fisherman. I drew him wearing a heavy, coarse blue and grey wool sweater. He lived near Mrs Sardia. Hannes subsequently died at sea.

ISHMAIL – Cass's father was short and fat, a Muslim hawker selling fruit and vegetables from a barrow near the Post Office. Ishmail and **MARELDIA**, Cass's mother, lived at the Seven Steps next to Motjie Ragmat.

JINX – He is in my painting of the British Cinema (Page 120) and was knifed to death for betraying DKs to another gang.

KAYE – Charlie's boyfriend and also a hairdresser.

LEONARD – The son of **MRS SCHOLZ**, who hid in bed with a bullet in his leg. I painted Mrs Sholtz's blue bathroom (Page 84).

MAANTJIE –The leader of the DKs often wore blue jeans with a broad black belt, a white shirt, and heavy jacket. **NAZIMA** was his wife.

MANNE – One of the DKs.

MENEER PRINS and **MENEER SMIT** – Warders at Roeland Street Prison.

MOTJIE RAGMAT KARRIEM – My dear friend and 'mother'. I came to know this family well – her daughter **AZIZA**, granddaughter **JULEIGA**, grandson **RASHIED**. Juleiga adored Motjie Ragmat. When Motjie was ill Juleiga would sleep on the floor next to her grandmother.

MR HARTLEY, THE TAILOR – His shop was at the entrance to Vernon Terrace. He and his assistant **OMAR** stored my equipment overnight when I was painting there.

MR FABER – A Jewish man who ran the National and British cinemas, as well as 'The Gem' in Woodstock.

MR LEZ FABER – Mr. Faber's son, who took over from his father. He stood with a revolver in his pocket when I was painting the *National Cinema at night* (Page 156).

MR JACKIE OAKER – Owned a barber shop. He sent children out with an umbrella to shelter me from the rain when I was painting. I had to finish the painting in his shop, and he moved practically everything to accommodate me. His son, **LIONEL OAKER**, also became a barber.

MR GOPAL VASSON – Original owner of Vasson's Shoe Shop in Hanover Street, and his sons **DALPIT** and **MOHAN**. A wonderful family whom I came to know well. They always fixed my shoes and were very kind to me.

MRS ALTHORPE – An old lady in the Old Age Home in District Six, who willingly sat for me.

MRS NELLIE HERBERT – She was Ernie's mother and they lived in Clifton Street. She and her two daughters were staunch Anglicans, who worshipped at St Mark's.

MRS MANSHUN – Lived in Vernon Terrace and saved my easel from being trampled by a runaway horse.

MRS SARDIA – Lived with her son in Mount Lane. She had a strong face and she was one of the first portraits I painted in District Six. She always wore a dress, apron, and doek tied around her head.

NICK – He and his wife ran the Court Lounge Restaurant, opposite the Supreme Court, where I often had meals. They were Greek.

OU VYF – He was a great friend of **MOTJIE RAGMAT KARRIEM**. He had the greenest eyes. He was thin, wore a long coat and always had one hand in the pocket. Did he only have five fingers in total, or did he lose five fingers on one of his hands in a fight? I never did find out. I knew that he dealt in dagga, had several wives and had been the head of a District Six gang.

RAY QUERIDO – A close and dear friend who was indebted to my father, Lee McGregor. She was a talented puppeteer.

SEPTEMBER – An old man in the District Six Old Age Home whom I painted.

SERGEANT DIRK VERMEULEN – A policeman whom I met on my first visit to Caledon Square.

STALAG 17s – They were a notorious gang - mostly in their twenties - who made their base at Winter Gardens, Ayre Street.

TALIEP PETERSEN AND DAVID KRAMER – Musicians, singers and actors.

THE OLD LADY in Miller's Fish & Chip shop, Hanover Street – this is where children would buy a few cents-worth of chips wrapped in neswpaper. I would stop in sometimes to buy fresh fish and then catch the bus home from the Seven Steps.

Appendix 3 – Loyal friends, forty years on

MOTJIE RAGMAT'S FAMILY
Sandra met Motjie Ragmat's daughter, Aziza Cassiem, and several members of her family, at the Kenilworth Centre in 2001. She knew all of Aziza's six children – Rashied, Juleiga, Gadija, Kulsom, Salaamah and Sadiah – and painted portraits of two of them, Juleiga and Rashied. The family lived with their grandmother, Motjie Ragmat in her house at the Seven Steps until 1972 when they moved to Athlone.

Like her mother, Aziza is deeply religious, and has made the Hadj twice, in 1988 and 1999. She starts everything she does with a prayer which she wrote down for Sandra:

> *Bis millah hier Ragmaan nier Rageem.*
> *We begin in the name of Allah the most gracious, the most merciful.*

Sandra was not forgotten by the family when Sadiah married and she was invited to the wedding.

> *I admired the women's long dresses of all different shades, and their beaded head-scarves, and felt completely at home in their company. When the bridal party arrived there was loud excitement as they made their way between the tables to the stage. In the retinue were a small girl and boy dressed exactly as the bride and groom. It was a lively and loving event, and for me a nostalgic highlight.*

CASS GORDON
Cass welcomed Sandra into his house, hugging her cheerfully and warmly. The walls of the entrance passage and sitting room were lined with paintings, but none of them were hers. Delicious smells were coming from the kitchen and Cass interrupted the conversation now and again to attend to several large pots simmering on the stove. Sandra and he reminisced enthusiastically about the old days in the District.

NAZIMA AHRENSE, MAANTJIE'S WIDOW
Meeting Sandra at the District Six Museum, Nazima spoke about her late husband, Abdurahman – nicknamed Maantjie from the 'man' at the end of his name – who was portrayed in Sandra's painting of the *National Cinema at night*. She told us how he could sing and play the guitar and had won

Aziza, Motjie Ragmat's daughter.

Sandra and Juleiga, Motjie Ragmat's granddaughter, whose portrait Sandra painted when she was a little girl.

Faldielah, Juleiga's daughter.

Sandra and Cass, whom Sandra painted many times, at his house in Walmer Estate.

Sandra and Nazima, Maantjie's widow.

Sandra and Gopal Vasson's grandson, Vinod.

Sandra and Fareed at the District Six Museum.

cups for the 'Coons'. Born in Caledon Street, he went to school in Prestwick Street, and then worked at the National Cinema, the British and the Star. When all the cinemas closed, Maantjie worked in the docks, and later for the local mosque.

Nazima was delighted to be given an enlarged photograph of Sandra's painting of the *National Cinema at night.*

THE VASSONS

Vinod Vasson's mother died in 1960, so her children lived with their father, Dalpit and uncle, Mohan and his family, six children in all. Dalpit and Mohan, schooled by their father as shoemakers, ran the shop, and brought up their children strictly. After school the children were obliged to return to the shop to help and learn the trade and the business. On Saturday when the shop closed at lunch time, they stayed on to clean the machines. Vinod's sisters worked in the house and were often called upon to help in a neighbouring grocery shop. Their strong Hindu faith was also an important part of their upbringing. The family loved the life of District Six, the warm, friendly community where people knew each other and mingled constantly.

With the bulldozers moving into the District, grandfather Gopal Vasson bought a shop in the Oriental Plaza in Woodstock. In 1973 the Vassons moved to Rylands on the Cape Flats. They occupy the same house today.

From his shop in Hanover Street Gopal could see buildings and mosques, the docks and a wonderful view of the sea. In the Oriental Plaza he had no view at all except for the material shop opposite. In Hanover Street there was sunshine and warmth; in the Plaza there was nothing but concrete and freezing cold in winter. It always resembled a morgue to me.

On the walls of their shop in the Oriental Plaza were photographs of District Six. Their customers came from Athlone, Lentegeur, Mitchell's Plain, Manenberg, Kensington, Retreat – all people who had once lived in the District.

Vinod, became articled to a firm of chartered accountants, B Fortes & Co and after qualifying remained with the firm for some years. Later he and two of his colleagues left to establish their own practice, where they still remain partners.

Sandra has never lost touch with this family, and when the two men whom Sandra knew best died, Mohan in 1994 and Dalpit in 1998, Sandra felt the loss deeply.

FAREED ROSSIER

In May 2009 the Road of Hope Gallery in Constantia called Fareed Rossier 'one of the more celebrated artists showcasing at the gallery at present.' All his paintings feature the design and culture of District Six. "Painting is my passion, my life," Fareed says. "Sandra McGregor inspired me and I will never give up."

List of Collectors

Libby Ardington
Steve Bales
Jessie Bosman
The District Six Museum, Cape Town
Malinda du Randt
Antony Fleischer
Dolores and Anthony Fleischer
Kevin Fleischer
Lance and Marie-Anne Fleischer
Maya Fleischer
R Bongani Fleischer
Spencer and Calla Fleischer
Sharon and Andy Griffin
Paul Hasse
John Hood
The Humbert Family Trust
Craig Jacobs
Debbie Jacobs
Hamish Jacobs
Vincent Kolbe
Angela Read Lloyd
Sandra McGregor
Ivor and Jennie Orchard
Sandra Prosalendis
The Very Rev Rowan Q Smith
John and Ros Stace
Kerry and Cheryl Swift
Mrs Elizabeth Stuart-Clark
Dr Stuart Young

List of Subscribers

Gary Adler
Julian Adler
Elisabeth and Peter Anderson
Alix and Tom Bothwell
Molly Buchanan
Mrs M Cabral
Edwin Cameron
Ant and Chesca
Mary and Brian Clarke
Rosemary and Peter Clarke
Michelle de Almeida
Mrs Angela Desmidt
The District Six Museum, Cape Town
Gail Dörje
Irene DuPont Library, St Andrew's School, Delaware, USA
Heather Edwards
Diane Fairhead
Christina Fleischer
Francesca Fleischer
Nicola Fleischer
Sophia Fleischer
Michael Hall
Peter and Janine Henderson
Catherine Horsfield
Harold Levy and Pat Sapinsley
Barbara Long-Innes
Malcolm and Cindy Long-Innes
Andrew and Megan Long-Innes
Ann Lorentz
Theo Lorentz
Kirsty Macfarlane
Ingrid and Neil Moir
David Porter
The Rev. Derek Pratt and Karen Pratt
Roedean School (SA)
Ruth CR Shannon
Hank Slack
Denise and Peter Solomon
South African Old Roedeanian Association (SAORA)
Naas Steenkamp
Lucy Stuart-Clark
Mary-Ann Wenham
Cindy Yeoman

About the author

Dolores Fleischer has been involved in research, editing, writing and production of books for many years. In 1995, on seeing a small photograph of a painting by Sandra McGregor, a school friend since childhood, she resolved to bring Sandra's story to life. Now, after extensive research, Dolores has written a deeply personal history of the artist and her work.

Dolores was born in Johannesburg and educated at Roedean and the University of the Witwatersrand. She has travelled extensively with her husband, Anthony, in Africa and abroad, living for some years in her beloved Portugal. They now live in Cape Town, their three sons and ten grandchildren scattered between South Africa, France and the USA.

END PAPERS

Street Plan, District Six

1. British Cinema
2. Rotten Row
3. National Cinema
4. Ayre Street
5. Caledon Street
6. Hanover Street
7. Seven Steps
8. Horsburg Lane
9. St Mark's Church
10. Muir Street Mosque
11. Clifton Street
12. Star Cinema
13. Aspeling Street
14. Aspeling Street Mosque
15. Dutch Reformed Church
16. Cross Street
17. Lee Street
18. Avalon Cinema

Sandra McGregor – 'Onse artist' in District Six